Lucy

CW01023299

The Wasted City
Approaches to
Circular City Making

Edited by
CITIES Foundation

trancity^xvaliz

Preface

We are living in an urban age, in which cities drive progress, growth and innovation all over the world. Such growth has consequences though, most visibly through the climate crisis, growing scarcity of natural resources, economic instability and social inequality. It has taken thousands of years for our cities to develop into the complex systems they are today, and now it is up to us to face the challenge of creating more healthy, prosperous and ultimately sustainable cities.

Cities have always been vulnerable. The early cities of Mesopotamia were deserted when the river basins shifted and there was no longer enough water available. Cities such as London, Birmingham and Manchester nearly collapsed because of the filth produced by capitalist practices in the 19th century. And it still holds true that cities that are not able to properly manage their water supply will be irretrievably lost, no matter how creative or economically successful they may be.

The material and biophysical aspects of the city (the materials and flows of water, waste and air) and the cultural and social order (how we cohabit) cannot be separated. This book takes this as its starting point and offers a refreshing collection of contributions that signify a new sort of emerging urban social movement. Taking issue with the linearity of modernist mass production,

it seeks to recoup a sense of urbanity that is both socially inclusive and limits waste.

The ingenious use and reuse of resources, from our daily habits to industrial manufacturing, presents a tangible example of how biophysical and cultural dimensions can interact productively.

The Wasted City puts forward the core concept of circular urbanism and its mobilizing potential to bring a future vision within reach. Ignoring the classic bottom-up and top-down dichotomy in a journey through neighbourhoods, cities and nations, the book not only primes our imagination for necessary, systemic circular change, but does so while taking a sharp look at the key judgements and actions of the pioneers of circularity. It helps us picture and imagine effective resource management, illustrated by interactions, transitions, operations and flows, where epochal changes happen slowly and citizens are more important than technologies.

One of the outstanding features of the book is that it constantly gives new meaning to the interaction of the biophysical and the cultural, the material and the people living in the urban realm. This book argues a clear case: citizens drive urban change—no matter how big or how small. From cities and their small communities to nations and their governments, today we need to anticipate and adapt to change in order to instil the right kind of long-

term ones. Producing a viable illustration of a new urban agenda that responds to the inabilities of traditional public policies by switching the governance focus to interconnected circular approaches acting on multiple levels, is a tool to elevate the discourse about systemic change via pragmatic interaction. The book is thoughtful and full of inspiration, and thus may well help give rise to the new focal point of a circular urbanism. This publication captures this perspective, depicts it, and provides a wealth of examples and approaches that serve as a springboard for dialogue and action about the future of our cities, which ultimately affects the future of all of us.

Maarten Hajer

Contents

The
Empowerment Plan
Detroit, USA
Page 60

Plant Chicago
Chicago, USA
Page 48

Toronto Tool Library
Toronto, Canada
Page 40

US BCSD
Austin, USA
Page 78

Brooklyn Microgrid
New York, USA
Page 19

Closed Loop Fund
New York, USA
Page 72

Circular Endeavour Case Studies

Essays on Policy Approaches

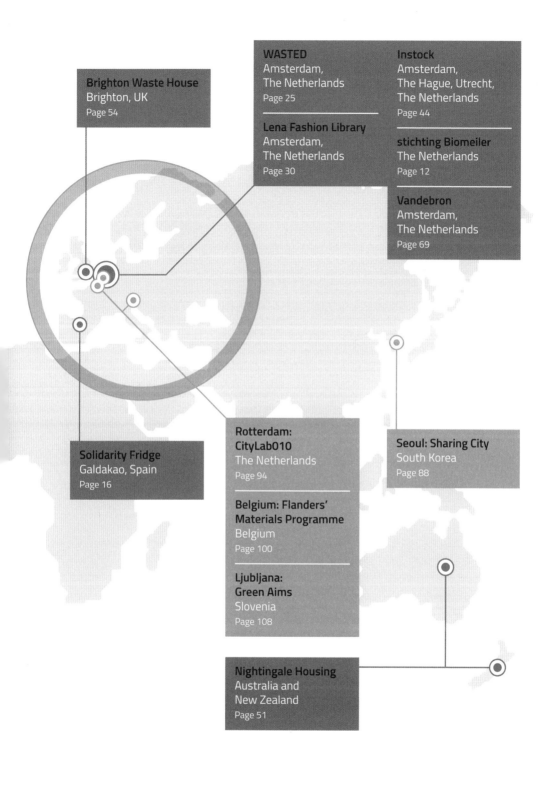

Introduction
Framing the
Wasted City

Francesca Miazzo
and Mehdi Comeau

CITIES Foundation

A city is a system, formed by the collective work of its interconnected people and parts. In today's cities, this system is linear—both economic interactions and socio-spatial developments are dominated by 'take-make-waste' habits. Decades in the making, this system slowly arose from an industrial make-and-consume boom. Excessive waste became standard, firmly embedded in our modes of operation and inescapable in our daily lives. The resulting city defies sustainable change, and defines the Wasted City: an urban settlement where it is difficult to develop circular systems on a mainstream basis. As opposed to linear, a circular system looks to re-integrate resources into the urban loop. Circulating rather than wasting serves to revitalize rather than deteriorate. This book interprets circularity as a comprehensive urban modus operandi. Achieving it challenges us to innovate, create and take action to disturb linearity at its roots. By freeing us from the Wasted City's grasp we can come closer to the circular city. But we cannot reach it. The truly circular city is utopian. It is an idealized vision for cities. Imagine, a city where nothing is wasted—where regenerative resource management spans built, social and natural environments. The urgency and ambition to create such sustainable urban futures is stronger than ever before. If you're paying attention, you see this uprising. You feel it. And circular urban systems appear to be well within reach. After all, technological advancements of the past few decades have given us tools for innovative progress. However, amid amplified efforts, cities remain dominantly linear, while circularity remains far from being mainstream. In part, what is missing is widespread, general commitment in circular progress. With such commitment, we hope comes the adoption of new, belief-backed habits by what we consider to be the most relevant agents of urban change: citizens. However, this is only part of the puzzle. It is one root of many that allows a complete circular urban system to flourish. This publication aims to shed light on these issues, bringing us all closer to circular urban realities. The connecting thread running through the book is a clear and simple path through a hazy and tangled urban transformation toward integrated, systems-level circularity. To start down this path, this book takes you through different scales, scopes and approaches. We analyse how citizens are involved as practitioners and co-owners of circular city initiatives. We dig deep into municipal strategies and learn from key national actors. And through several opinion pieces, we discover how metabolism, socio-spatial relationships and cultural change all play a role in systemic change— in collectively overcoming the challenges of today's Wasted City.

The book is written for professionals, academics, students and urban enthusiasts. Best suited for those who are already acquainted with concepts such as urban metabolism, a focus on methodologies and best practices offers constructive insight. We write from a future perspective, where collective ownership and management of the urban process override the privately owned development of linear urban artefacts. To help realize such a future, this book offers insights readers can use to engage in constructive dialogue. Let us first begin by explaining our standpoint. Looking at the city as an ecosystem, urban planning, design and architectural practices adapt the built environment in which people interact as organisms within a complex system. We see grand opportunities for planners to reinterpret the landscape and act in a more inclusive, cooperative fashion that propagates sustainable economic activity and vigorous cultural strength. Urban professionals, however, are not the only city makers actively shaping cities we inhabit. Increasingly, diverse actors from citizens to creative entrepreneurs, governments, lobbies and companies are entering the field of sustainable urban development. We observe an increasing amount of cross-sector, co-creational initiatives for urban process management. These new-found and emerging methods accelerate the integration of circular practices in cities, developing a new level of collective socio-spatial urban ownership. We see such stimulation through our own practice. CITIES Foundation has researched, developed and implemented multiple research-based publications, local projects and social enterprises, which all provide more circular, sustainable and community-led city-making approaches. Each initiative comes with multi-actor, cross-sector collaboration that forms around the co-management with the final users of sustainable practices. Based on our experiences and practical examples, this publication aims to advance a new standard of circular city making that roots academic, professional and informal citizen thinking and action in an effective process that begins and ends with people, with the goal of bringing this discourse to impact a more mainstream public.

A Journey into the Virtuous Circular Spiral

From working, operating and researching the field of circular city making with a focus on people-driven change in socio-spatial environments at CITIES Foundation, we organized this book as a journey into the virtuous circular spiral. On the route we take examining cases from the hyper-local to the city, regional and national level, a select group of specialised individuals working directly with CITIES' international team complete Part One. In Part Two, we welcome external professionals, experts and thinkers engaged in the field of circularity to contribute their personal insights. The book's focus is on the global north, with most of the attention directed at Northern Europe and the USA. On this journey, the circular city does not simply equate re-use; we look at the complicated agglomerations of fluxes, people and operations that are driving re-industrialization, are empowering sharing economies based on co-ownership and co-management, and are inspiring strategies that contribute to creating profound change in the long run. This book brings such strategies to the forefront, working as a tool to feed discussions that lead to the further development of circular cities—not as an end, but as a means for systemic change.

In Part One, we begin by presenting a variety of novel strategies in *An Array of Circular Endeavours*. Composed of 16 case study reviews, this chapter brings you in touch with existing initiatives that are breaking the linear mould. We bolstered knowledge about each case through one-on-one interviews with the initiators—inspired citizens who are driven by the purpose and potential of transforming linear processes into circular ones. The range of approaches spans the voluntary allocation of public fridges to prevent food waste and the re-industrialization of Detroit, to nation-wide energy providers and material-exchange initiatives. These examples highlight an important point: there is no single recipe for circularity; it is approached from different angles and perspectives, on varying scales. Anyone can select certain tools from the box and apply them to an issue in their own way. Yet no one circular act is isolated—a combination of singular initiatives holds the potential for achieving shared goals on a large scale. But this requires the adoption of new methods at a higher level. As we discussed in our 2014 book, *We Own The City*, a progressive, ingenious institutional environment is necessary to enable a systemic change at the city level. Consequently, the book follows this line of thinking in the section *Circular City: A Selection of Policy Approaches*, where we present a series of inspiring urban and regional administrations that are experimenting with what the circular city is or can be. What is engrossing about this chapter is that every administration applies a very different, context-based set of solutions, highlighting that at the level of city administration best approaches to circular city making remain undefined. From Seoul, South Korea to Flanders, Belgium, Rotterdam, the Netherlands and Ljubljana, Slovenia, chapter two shows a very palpable reality, where circular city making is far from being mainstream because ventures in circularity still spring from experimental approaches. At the national level, it is time to start implementing regulatory reforms that allow, enable and support circular activities going forward. We explore this interplay in the last chapter of Part One, *The Role of National Government in Circular City Making*, learning how the national level serves as an appropriate arena to jump-start circular regulatory reforms. To gain insight, we interviewed two civil servants from the Netherlands and Sweden. As with all chapters in Part One, we conclude with a narrated summary of the findings that overall provide a clear story throughout the discoveries of our travel through the spiral of circular city making.

In Part Two, our findings are met with a series of opinion pieces on circularity, written by individuals with varied, relevant experiences with and connections to circular city making. First, Konstantinos Kourkoutas and Federico Savini discuss the circular city using Amsterdam and Barcelona as inspirational contexts to generalize about issues of metabolism and socio-economic transitions. Then Michiel Schwarz elaborates on the cultural challenge that we face while opting for a circular urbanity, and last but not least, Joost Beunderman provides a motivating yet practical overview of realistic steps that lead us to comprehensive systemic change. This final piece represents the true conclusion of this publication, where Joost provides a synthesis of his extensive experience in developing, conceptualizing and debating on the 'massive change' needed to bring urban circularity to a more established position. The concluding remarks depict our discoveries, generalized into a set of statements. These statements are the final beliefs we will stand behind when presenting this publication. Our final goal is not to define a beginning and an end of circular city making. Instead, we intend to kick-start a journey that will continue in the real world—where together with other circular city makers, we will debate, discuss and take our ambition forward, bringing this bulk of knowledge to more people and more areas, moving closer to collective, systemic urban circularity.

Part One
Travelling Through
the Circular Spiral

An Array of Circular Endeavours

Alex Thibadoux
CITIES Foundation

Introduction

Contemporary urban existence depends on a tangle of materials, processes, operations and behaviours, which are mostly unseen and unknown. The luxury of taking for granted such essential complexities is characteristic of many cities, and it enables residents to concentrate on matters far more advanced than food and shelter. considering how intricate and connected this tangle is, it is quite difficult for cities to develop or implement change-based solutions in a timely manner. As growing populations compete for a shrinking pool of resources worldwide, an increasing majority of people is living in cities. This makes cities places of challenge and opportunity, ideally suited to not only find solutions that minimize foreign inputs and waste, but also to experiment with people and processes.

Part One shows how the transition to a circular city requires new approaches to city making, and cooperation from a wide range of actors across diverse sectors of society. We analyse cases that reveal how consumption must evolve into new types of producer-consumer relationships in order to support material lifecycles and production from renewable sources. All this affects the foundations of urbanity: housing, food, and energy, as well as more nuanced aspects of manufacturing and retail. With such a widespread and interconnected challenge at hand, it is difficult to know how or where to begin. This part of the book is designed to help. Each case is examined in an effort to understand how the circular city might look and function in the future and to identify what obstacles are currently in the way, in order to help devise strong solutions going forward. Our selection of cases varies widely in scale and strategy, but they are united by innovation and a determination to improve the way we use and manage resources necessary to sustain life. Most of the examples are born from forward-thinking citizens with a purpose for change, while several examples feature semi-private or hybrid ventures that rethink the logic of profit in a circular way. Other examples touch upon wider issues, such as unemployment, homelessness and education. Regardless of the focus, initiator or support network, all cases in this book are reactions to outdated, common, linear customs that in turn face financial, political, or cultural barriers that stymie their growth. Together, they represent a present-day snapshot of practices, ideas and methods that close material loops and engage citizens in moving towards systemic change.

Get ready to take your first steps into a journey through circular city making. To ensure smooth travel, cases are organized in order of size—moving from hyper-local, citizen-led revolutions up to nation-wide corporate agreements. We cannot classify any as small-scale or bottom-up, as these definitions are too linear and imply a dichotomy that does not represent the complicated matrix needed for circularity to flourish. The full classification of cases will be presented in our concluding remarks, where we evaluate our findings.

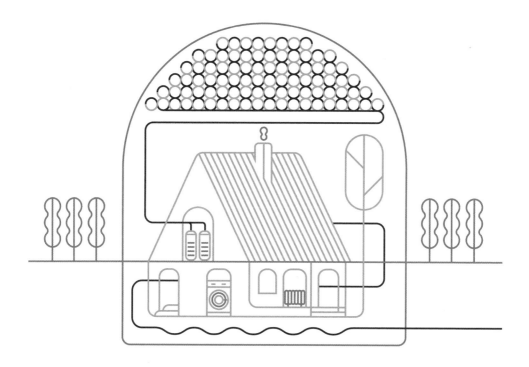

stichting Biomeiler

66 We are mostly interested in research and experimentation.

— Frank Scholtens

Year started
2014

Type
Volunteer organization

Location
The Netherlands

Industry
Energy

Category
Renewable energy, off-grid

Founders
Peter Jan Brouwer, Frank Scholtens and Arie van Ziel

Website
biomeiler.nl

A successful,
group-built biomeiler.

We all need to keep warm. While essential, it calls for massive energy. Just think about heat and hot water at your own home. Collectively across Europe, heating is estimated to consume 70% of energy use in residential buildings. Mainly powered by fossil fuels (coal, oil, natural gas), innovations in heating technology could generate a remarkable reduction in energy consumption. Imagine if cities could be heated from organic, locally produced inputs. A biomeiler is a low-tech system that captures heat from compost, capable of producing continuous warmth for years on end.

Stichting Biomeiler is a volunteer-operated non-profit organization dedicated to sharing knowledge around biomeilers, and assisting in their construction throughout the Netherlands. The technology functions on the same principles as traditional composting, with aerobic bacteria breaking down organic matter and releasing heat. By running water-filled piping through wood chips, reliable heat can be generated on almost any off-grid site, with a by-product of high-quality compost that also binds CO_2 to reduce greenhouse gases in the atmosphere. Biomeiler technology has been in use for decades, but has remained an alternative energy method. It did however gain some traction after the turn of the twenty-first century, propelled by a group of enthusiasts who started

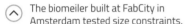
The biomeiler built at FabCity in Amsterdam tested size constraints.

Arie van Ziel working with compost by-product.

Native Power in Germany, and the online streaming of pioneering videos made by the French inventor Jean Pain.

There are two main challenges of operating biomeilers in a city. First, they require land. What is likely the smallest biomeiler in the Netherlands was recently built at Fab City Campus, a temporary micro society constructed to explore innovation and creativity in Europe. While the 2.5-meter high, 2-meter wide construction proved capable of producing temperatures of 45–50C (113–120F) inside, most cities do not have enough space for these constructions to be common. Additionally, the biomass required to generate heat, particularly wood chips, would be difficult to generate in substantial quantities for urban environments.

Research and experimentation with the technology to power improvements is a major goal of stichting Biomeiler, and as an open-source foundation, they freely share all their ideas and findings. In the future, they would like to set up systems to test the suitability of additional organic waste streams. While biomeilers are perhaps currently best suited for rural applications, they can provide temporary, off-grid heating in cities. Low-tech solutions should not be overlooked in the quest for sustainable energy and circular city making. To refine development and

⌃ Children testing water
heated by a biomeiler.

adapt biomeiler technology to better suit
and serve urban environments, additional
research still needs to be conducted.

⊕ Pros
Clean heating produced from
organic materials.

⊖ Cons
Requires large quantities
of biomass and land.

→ Takeaway
Research into low-tech energy
solutions could produce big benefits.

Solidarity Fridge (Nevera Solidaria©)

66 We are aware that this is not the solution, but it is a step. These little things are the things that change life, that change our reality.

— Ainhoa Crespo Gadea
Solidarity Fridge team

Year started
2015

Type
Non-profit volunteer organization

Location
Galdakao, Basque Country, Spain

Industry
Food

Category
Resource management,
food waste

Founders
Alvaro Saiz and Galdakaoko
Boluntarioen Gizarte Elkartea

Website
neverasolidaria.org

A small fence around it helps to secure the fridge's place on the street.

Uneaten food is a major environmental and economic problem in cities. For starters, the water and energy required to grow and transport food is wasted when the end product is wasted, while decomposing food waste in landfills creates methane—a heat-trapping greenhouse gas significantly more damaging than CO_2. While this is a global issue concentrated in cities, all food waste ends up being a local issue. And the local level is exactly where Solidarity Fridge steps in to tackle the issue with a simple intervention: providing community refrigerators where anyone can take or leave donated surplus food.

In the village of Galdakao, located outside of Bilbao in the Basque Country of northern Spain, Solidarity Fridge was an inventive response to a troubling law that banned volunteer associations from giving away fresh food, and to the startling amount of edible food being wasted. As local volunteer associations were restricted, food waste multiplied. The founders of Solidarity Fridge presented their solution to the local city council, which was surprisingly supportive and allowed a three-month pilot programme to kick off. In just the first month, about 440 lbs (200 kg) of food was saved. Today, they have helped organize more than ten fridges across Spain, with additional installations in the works in Argentina and

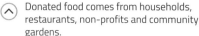

Donated food comes from households, restaurants, non-profits and community gardens.

Mexico. As part of the charity organization Galdakaoko Boluntarioen Gizarte Elkartea (GBGE), Solidarity Fridge relies on a network of volunteers to establish and maintain projects in new communities. Generally, the refrigerators are second-hand, donated to support the cause. A certified electrician volunteers time to sign off on the electrical connection, and approximately one hundred volunteers are involved throughout the country to carry out daily operations.

As a community tool to curb food waste, Solidarity Fridge is open to everyone, regardless of social standing, which makes their approach quite different from charitable food banks. It also reduces stigma and encourages participation from anyone and everyone in the area. When presenting the idea to a new community, there is often a fear that the appliance or its contents could be vandalized or sabotaged, but with approximately two years in operation, there have been no instances of such hostility. Within a municipality there are usually two approvals necessary to install the fridge. First, the city council must allow the public occupation of sidewalk space. Next, Health Services must sign off on the project. To comply, food is labelled with dates of preparation and no raw meat is allowed. To keep things fresh and clean, volunteers regularly clean the fridges and take out old goods. With a slogan translated to 'One Neighbourhood, One Fridge', Solidarity Fridge understands that community fridges are a small, localized solution to a much more endemic problem. However, within an appropriate neighbourhood context, they offer immediate accommodation for food that would otherwise be wasted. This analogue approach proves that with initiative and a dash of ingenuity, impact can be generated from the ground up on a small scale.

Brooklyn Microgrid

66 The plan is to continue developing Brooklyn Microgrid to the point we can actually sell a majority share in it to the community members and community organizations, so that it is truly a community-run organization.

— Scott Kessler
Director of Business Development

Year started
2016

Type
For-profit social enterprise

Location
Brooklyn, New York, USA

Industry
Energy, utilities

Category
Renewable energy, block chain

Founders
LO3 Energy; Lawrence Orsini

Website
brooklynmicrogrid.com

Lawrence Orsini installing a TransActive
Grid e-meter in a Brooklyn Microgrid
participant's home.

Cities are largely dependent on energy
that is generated great distances away.
This is not only inefficient, but also
makes communities vulnerable when
they rely solely on imported power.
In 2012, Hurricane Sandy caused
widespread power outages in New York
City and beyond. Failures within the
inter-connected power grid left millions
without electricity. Reorganizing the way
electricity is generated and distributed
can make cities more self-sufficient
and robust, at the same time providing
economic opportunities for citizens.

A microgrid is a small type of utility
grid that can operate independently
or alongside a larger power network.

Brooklyn Microgrid is developing and
testing these systems in three New York
City neighbourhoods. Utilizing blockchain
technology, they are building a peer-to-
peer marketplace for hyper-local green
energy transactions. Blockchain is a
digital ledger that simultaneously shares,
updates, and distributes information
without the need for a central storage
facility for data. This enables peer-to-
peer transactions with both parties
privy to the exact same information,
eliminating the need for the usual retail
energy intermediary, and enabling energy
producers to sell directly to consumers.
Brooklyn Microgrid is providing forty
households in the Boerum Hill, Gowanus
and Park Slope neighbourhoods with

A Brooklyn Microgrid
participant's rooftop.

Walking tour of Brooklyn Microgrid
photovoltaic installation with
installer and architect.

the equipment necessary for this energy exchange.

By decentralizing energy production and distribution, Brooklyn Microgrid is creating economic and environmental incentive for neighbourhood level green energy investment. For the first time in New York City, homeowners can sell the excess energy that they generate, and consumers can choose the source of their energy supply, which could be right across the street. This new potential revenue stream should help drive outside investment in neighbourhood energy production infrastructure. This local energy also increases overall energy efficiencies. Every time a transformer or substation is

used, electrons are lost. In a local energy marketplace, value can be placed on energy productivity, encouraging energy to travel the most effective pathways. Currently, green energy is often produced a great distance away from where it is consumed. Localizing and condensing energy networks can achieve greater energy productivity and decrease overall demand.

Brooklyn Microgrid has developed a hyper-local solution that uses new technology to empower residents and potentially power cities like never before. When citizens take control of generating and distributing electricity, they can reap economic and environmental

A wall of TransActive Grid e-meters
in the testing laboratory.

benefits unavailable with traditional
energy networks. A matrix of microgrids
across urban environments could be
the adaptable infrastructure required to
propel cities forward from within.

+ Pros
Creates incentive for local green
energy investment, while building
on existing infrastructure.

− Cons
Potentially difficult to operate
within traditional utility systems
and regulations.

→ Takeaway
New technology can enable
hyper-local energy production
and transactions.

WASTED

66 WASTED was born following our method at CITIES: we asked citizens and the local support network about their needs and ambitions for the neighbourhood, then developed a solution everybody can be a part of, where plastic recycling is a means not an end.

— Francesca Miazzo
  Director

Year started
2015

Type
Non-profit organization

Location
Amsterdam, the Netherlands

Industry
Recycling

Category
Recycling, resource management

Founders
CITIES Foundation

Website
wastedlab.nl

Building blocks made from locally collected, melted and reprocessed plastic.

Plastic is a fascinating substance. Originally, it was used as a more affordable alternative to wood and ivory. Now being a commercial material for just over 100 years, its continued success in countless applications has rendered it omnipresent in everyday life. Ultimately, plastic gave rise to mass consumerism as it made more and more products available to more and more people. But plastic's success in the consumer realm also led to widespread use of single-use products and much waste. As plastics are generally oil-based and rarely recycled, the ensuing environmental challenges are formidable. This is common knowledge; however, it appears that few consumers are motivated to change their consumption patterns. WASTED set out to change this.

Based in the northern district of Amsterdam, WASTED is centred on a reward system that functions as an incentive programme to promote recycling behaviour and awareness in the neighbourhood. In practice, WASTED participants receive one plastic coin for each bag of plastic they recycle. The coins can be used at over thirty local shops and cultural organizations for freebies and discounts. Initial enrolment in the reward system's first year surpassed 700 households. On average, participants separated 70% of their plastic, 52% said they started changing waste disposal

WASTED coins can be exchanged for discounts on local goods and services.

habits because of the programme and 23% reduced their plastic consumption. In addition to the reward system, hands-on educational programmes are offered to schools and non-profits. This combination of outreach, education, and incentive was effective in influencing the actions of this pilot group.

In the project's early first phase, WASTED collected plastic waste from the neighbourhood to transform it into modular building blocks. They partnered with designers to develop a mobile lab capable of melting plastic into 4x4 inch (10x10 cm) cubes. The blocks were used to construct local tree planters and street furniture, but they proved to be

a difficult building component. The lab now demonstrates the transformative potential of plastic as a local resource and challenges people to consider the origin and final destination of the plastic used in their daily lives. The next phase of the programme, 2WASTED, will digitize the reward scheme with an app, expanding the programme to more participants and benefits.

Today, companies, designers, and municipalities do have the industrial capability to recycle most types of plastics, however there is not enough motivation across the board to make closed-loop systems a reality. WASTED promotes this vision with on-the-ground

<(Student reshaping plastic into blocks
     during an educational workshop.

^) WASTED programme
     plastic drop-off point.

action, transforming the mundane (and
generally unappreciated) task of recycling
into a process with tangible benefits and
results. This spurs a new social contract
that has the capacity to educate and
empower, ultimately instilling behaviour
that is critical for a circular future.

(+) Pros
      Reward scheme increases recycling
      and reduces consumption.

(−) Cons
      Difficult to implement and change
      established cultural protocol.

(→) Takeaway
      Educating and empowering local
      residents can induce system level
      change.

LENA the fashion library

66 The total value of one product is much greater than one sale. We hope to convince more brands to join.

– Elisa Jansen
Co-Founder

Year started
2014

Type
For-profit social enterprise

Location
Amsterdam, the Netherlands

Industry
Clothing

Category
Resource management, sharing economy, library, retail

Founders
Angela Jansen, Diana Jansen, Elisa Jansen and Suzanne Smulders

Website
lena-library.com

LENA the fashion
library's founders.

When we think about bettering our world, we don't usually think about our clothes. Yet the clothing industry is a terrible polluter, creating cheap goods that are mostly sold, bought and thrown out in cities. In approaching a circular city, can we refashion this wasteful system and still keep our outfits in style? Founded by three sisters and a friend, LENA the fashion library is both a clothing store and a service that lends out clothing to a network of members, much like books from a traditional library. Utilizing the sharing economy, their quality garments can be worn a greater number of times, lowering overall clothing consumption. By providing access to a collection of durable garments, LENA aims to be a resource for more sustainable fashion.

For many, a wardrobe is created and sustained by purchasing low-cost, low-quality clothing articles. consumers benefit from the affordable price and quick turnaround of 'fast fashion', but they are typically shielded from the undesirable effects of their shopping. These can include extensive use of land, water, pesticides and chemicals, worker exploitation, material waste and a slew of environmental impacts at each step of the product chain. And to top it off, many clothing articles are worn infrequently, which is effectively a waste.

Clothes for lending include vintage and designer labels.

As a for-profit social enterprise in the fashion industry, LENA the fashion library does not fit the typical profile of a business focused on sustainability. This presents a challenge in terms of funding models and customer retention. Most clothing shoppers are not used to the idea of regularly returning to a store to buy or borrow clothes. LENA has found that even enthusiastic supporters of their idea have cancelled their subscription because they can't make time to stop by. Since it is proving difficult to change consumer behaviour, they are adapting by developing an online platform to complement the physical store. Shoppers will be able to order online and pick up

the clothes either at the shop, designated pickup points, or through the post.

By increasing access to clothing and providing alternatives to ownership, LENA is lessening the environmental impact of the fashion industry. They aim to help facilitate other lending libraries through advice and the application of their self-developed lending library software, which has the potential to cross over into other sectors of the sharing economy. The quickest change can be achieved if others replicate LENA's lending model, if it spreads and more consumers support it with intent to reduce the impact of the products and services they use. The circular city will require more consumers

 Opening night
celebration.

to modify their behaviour and for more
businesses to experiment with new
models of operation.

⊕ Pros
Waste from the fashion industry can
be minimized, while creating access
to quality products.

⊖ Cons
Could prove difficult to implement
on a larger scale (more sizes, styles,
tracking, et cetera).

→ Takeaway
It is not easy to change consumer
behaviour, but creating a replicable
model helps.

Library of Things

66 One of the main reasons we have a physical place, rather than it just being digital, is that we believe that people have to experience something tangibly in order to be able to understand what it can do for them. If you want to create real change and reach groups that aren't usually reached, you have to have a physical space.

— Sophia Wyatt, *Director*

Year started
2014

Type
Non-profit

Location
London, UK

Industry
Consumer goods

Category
Sharing economy, library, social enterprise

Founders
Rebecca 'Bex' Trevalyan, Sophia Wyatt, Emma Shaw, and James Tattersfield

Website
libraryofthings.co.uk

Borrowers checking
out a waffle iron.

Inside the shipping container
that houses the library.

Cities are filled with an ever-expanding collection of consumer goods, but how much stuff do we really need to own? In a circular city, citizens should optimally utilize materials, components and products; owning too many underused items is simply uneconomical and rather foolish. One way to reduce material consumption is to borrow products that one doesn't use very often. Take, for example, the sharing economy's iconic power drill (more on power tools in the following case study), which most people usually use only for minutes but owns for years. Library of Things gathers useful items, such as drills, and with the support of its neighbours, is creating more with less.

At Library of Things, members can borrow a wide range of items as diverse as camping supplies, kitchen equipment and musical instruments. Items that are only needed once in a while, like a PA system, are rented to members at a low price. In addition, those with a DIY inclination can receive one-on-one instruction or attend workshops to learn how to use things such as power tools and sewing machines. In short, everyone can access useful items that may be rarely needed or too expensive to buy. It also offers a way to explore new hobbies or crafts without material commitment.

Organized as a non-profit, Library of Things is a people-focused community project. Beyond the core team of founders, they rely on volunteers to help run the library, conduct community outreach and keep products in good condition. After a successful pilot in a public library and months of searching, Library of Things found a more permanent location. Operating out of a pair of retrofitted shipping containers adjacent to a food surplus supermarket and regional recycling centre, they help round out a small community of resource-savvy organizations. The space is a place to meet neighbours and exchange knowledge on how to use different items.

As Library of Things matures, it aims to be a community-owned business that is flexible enough to adapt to the needs of any local population. By offering a toolkit and boot camp to others, they hope to create and share a replicable model for other interested communities. In libraries fitting this model, profit and ownership are not the main drivers of commodity utilization. With people able to borrow instead of buy, access to goods is decoupled from an increase in resource consumption. This new social contract encourages community, knowledge sharing and collaborative consumption in lieu of conventional ownership.

⟨ The Library of
Things' founders.

⊕ Pros
Reduces resource consumption
and associated waste, encourages
community activity.

⊖ Cons
It can be difficult to find and maintain
an affordable space.

→ Takeaway
Ownership and profit do not have
to be the main drivers of commodity
utilization, and access can overrule
ownership.

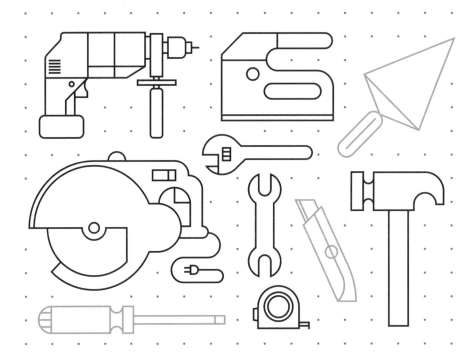

Toronto Tool Library

66 The default is to go out and buy something, right? So we are trying to tell people 'Don't do that. It is a waste of money. It is terrible for the environment to keep on doing that. So why don't you just share instead?'

— Ryan Dyment
Co-Founder & Executive Director

Year started
2013

Type
Non-profit

Location
Toronto, Canada

Industry
Consumer goods

Category
Resource management, library, retail, sharing economy

Founders
Lawrence Alvarez, Ryan Dyment

Website
torontotoollibrary.com/our-story/

There are over 5,000 tools
in the library system.

The construction and maintenance required to keep cities functioning is not limited to large-scale infrastructure. Inside every dwelling a variety of home improvement and personal projects requires an assortment of tools. For non-professionals, sharing these tools makes economic and environmental sense; consumers can save money by not purchasing items that they will only occasionally use and the tools in circulation can be used much more often. The Toronto Tool Library offers neighbours the opportunity to borrow a wide variety of tools to improve their home or community space.

Since opening in 2013, The Toronto Tool Library has grown to 5,000 tools and four different locations, experimenting with different sizes and partnerships. In addition to two storefront locations, one branch is situated in a public library, and another smaller outpost shares a building with a community makerspace. At one of their larger locations, they also run their own makerspace, providing access to a wood shop, laser cutter and 3D printers. The tool library provides after-school programmes and workshops that teach tool and technology use. Toronto Tool Library plans to expand into condos and co-op buildings next, where residential density is apt to support such a service.

Members use the wood shop to work on projects.

With real estate prices in the city continually rising, finding affordable space is the greatest challenge of the tool library. Membership prices are set low in order to provide financial incentive to join, but even with a mostly volunteer staff and a majority of donated tools, competing to pay for market-rate rent proves difficult. As a result, without partnerships, operating out of basement spaces and locations in less desirable areas is the reality.

The Toronto Tool Library hopes to be a part of a larger network in the future. If the library model becomes the standard practice for tool usage in cities, then the manufacturing process for tools could be reimagined. Currently many consumer tools are of low quality and difficult to repair. They are designed to be low-cost and discarded when broken. With incentive, tool manufacturers could produce items designed for longevity. Higher upfront costs would be recovered with an extended lifecycle and material wastes could be greatly reduced.

Lending libraries can serve an important function in the circular future. They lessen consumer impact while increasing access to goods and services. With accessible locations in the city, they can provide a network of community spaces, where citizens can learn from one another and share resources. Ensuring room in the city

(∧) The makerspace is an accessible
innovation and technology hub.

for these operations is a facilitative step
toward more resourceful habits.

(+) Pros
Community spaces where knowledge
and materials are shared.

(−) Cons
Difficult to finance in a free market.

(→) Takeaway
Partnerships with other non-profit or
civic organizations may be necessary
to generate new city services.

Instock

66 We want to enable other restaurants and caterers to also join us in our battle against food waste. All actors in the chain need to proactively work together to tackle this issue.

— Selma Seddik
  Co-Founder

Year started
2014

Type
Non-profit foundation/social enterprise

Locations
Amsterdam, The Hague and Utrecht

Industry
Food, service

Category
Food waste, restaurants, super-markets, new business models

Founders
Selma Seddik, Merel Laarman, Bart Roetert, and Freke van Nimwegen

Website
instock.nl

A worker picking up produce for the restaurant.

Instock serves breakfast, lunch, and dinner utilizing surplus foods.

Food waste is a massive source of misspent energy and resources. With estimates that a whopping 30–40% of food produced in many countries goes unused, tackling this complex issue should be a top priority for communities that wish to be more self-sufficient. Instock focuses on a specific food waste stream that is easy to overlook: supermarkets. Capturing and redirecting the waste, they collect these would-be-wasted commodities to use as ingredients at their restaurants.

Instock was born out of an innovation competition at Ahold Delhaize, a large food retail group with supermarket chains and convenience stores in Europe, the USA and beyond. Four colleagues at Ahold and Albert Heijn, a sizable subsidiary grocery store chain, proposed a business plan to reduce food waste through the creation of restaurants. They now daily collect food surplus from Albert Heijn grocery stores to use in one of their restaurant locations. The menu changes every day, based on what is available. In addition, they have developed a cookbook to help others use the bits of ingredients often leftover in the fridge and have partnered with Brouwerij Troost, a brewery in Amsterdam, to produce Pieper Bier, the first 'waste-made beer' in the Netherlands that incorporates leftover potatoes from the grocery store and suppliers.

⌃ Some of the Instock
  kitchen staff.

Organized as a non-profit foundation, Instock receives initial funding to set up each restaurant from Albert Heijn, with the goal of eventually making each location run self-sufficiently. This localized model, with a large supermarket chain as both financier and stocker, appears to be working well. Instock has grown to three locations with approximately one hundred employees in just over two years. For now, Instock is satisfied with this growth and has no immediate plans to open additional locations. Instead, they would like to focus on their current operations. Currently, the Instock restaurants are saving approximately 220, 460 lbs (100,000 kg) of supermarket food from being wasted each year. In the future, they would like to help other organizations work with food waste, hoping to pave the way for more caterers and restaurants to use food surplus, and to possibly provide it themselves.

Grocery stores are in a unique position to proactively and creatively manage their food waste streams. The Instock model is a local solution that may be challenging to implement elsewhere, as it requires substantial initial capital. However, their growth, success and financial backing suggest that great potential exists for a previously highly under-utilized resource: supermarket surplus.

Pieper beer is made
from waste potatoes

Pros
Successful, creative strategy
to divert food waste.

Cons
Requires considerable investment.

Takeaway
Supermarket food waste can
be salvaged with a plan to use
it elsewhere.

Plant Chicago

66 We're working to make our cities healthier and more efficient by developing and sharing the most innovative methods for sustainable food production, energy conservation and material reuse.

— Jonathan Pereira
Executive Director

Year started
2011

Type
Non-profit/profit partnership

Location
Chicago, USA

Industry
Food

Categories
Food production, manufacturing, closed loop

Founder
John Edel

Website
plantchicago.org

Food production methods have dramatically evolved over the past few centuries. Machine-dominated mega farms that ship products over great distances have largely replaced labour-intensive, local and family-run farms. The latter practices use nearby resources to produce higher quality food for local populations. Renewed interest in this type of local food production aligns with circular city making concepts, and Plant Chicago pushes things forward by partnering on a project called The Plant, a closed-loop, collaborative community of food businesses under one roof in the middle of Chicago, America's third largest city.

Located in a former meatpacking facility built in 1925, The Plant currently hosts operations for over a dozen food businesses that produce everything from micro greens to bread, beer and kombucha. Plant Chicago seeks to connect the waste streams from these operations, creating a beneficial closed-loop system. By establishing a community of vertical integration, they are creating a new business model based on community, urban agriculture and shared resources. Plant Chicago is a non-profit that partners with the developer of the building and the businesses sharing a location at The Plant. As food enterprises are established in the building, Plant

Chicago incentivizes and facilitates waste flows between different operations.

The most abundant material flow in The Plant is spent grain produced from the Whiner Beer Co. brewery. Plant Chicago is performing an ongoing series of experiments to create biomass briquettes from the used grains. The intention is to produce combustible fuel that can serve as substitute for firewood at Pleasant House Bakery, another tenant in the building. In addition, an in-house anaerobic digester is under construction. When completed, every day it will be able to process up to 16 tons of food waste that is hard to use for other purposes, coming from both on- and off-site suppliers. The machine will create biogas that can offset the use of natural gas on-site, helping to power businesses, such as the brewery, with their own waste.

The organizational model at Plant Chicago has great potential. Small businesses on site can develop symbiotic relationships that create economic benefits through cooperation with each other and by operating as part of a larger collective with a built-in marketplace. With educational and community engagement components, The Plant offers their urban neighbours a chance to experience local food first-hand. However, developing a comprehensive revenue model is a challenge, as The Plant includes operations from a number of different businesses. As a non-profit that runs education programmes, research, and a year-round farmers market, Plant Chicago relies on yearly foundation funding that is time consuming to manage. For small for-profit food businesses, profit margins are relatively low. Now that The Plant is beginning to mature into a closed-loop urban food production community of multiple businesses, the hope is that a rising tide will lift all boats, and all will share in the success of a budding, local circular economy.

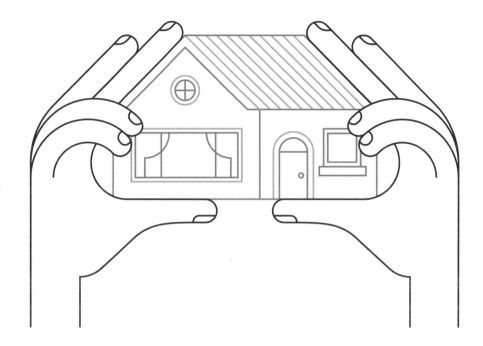

Nightingale Housing

As the world's population continues funnelling into urban areas, many cities are experiencing a real estate boom with rising prices and widespread development. Typically, developer-driven housing construction aims for low cost and maximum profit. This equation often produces dubious quality with environmental, social, and economic implications. As urban centres build, rebuild and expand, there is an opportunity to create housing in line with sustainable, circular city making practices: using appropriate materials to make low-energy, high-quality dwellings that enable citizens to engage with each other, and the city, in a minimal impact environment. Nightingale Housing attempts to upend the typical hierarchy of urban residential development with a new model that spurs sustainable, affordable homes.

A non-profit that connects progressive architects, investors, and owner-occupied home buyers to produce

Year started
2014

Type
Non-profit social enterprise

Location
Australia and New Zealand

Industry
Construction, architecture

Category
Architecture, co-housing

Founders
Breathe Architecture

Website
nightingalehousing.org

Nightingale 1 resident
site meeting.

multi-family residential co-housing, Nightingale Housing upholds a triple bottom line: social, environmental and financial sustainability. By capping project profits (currently at 15% of total project costs) and incorporating economic material design, they are able to create housing at below-market rates. Community facilities such as rooftop gardens and laundry encourage interaction while providing environmental benefits. In the prototypical development called The Commons, energy conservation is achieved with a design that eliminates air conditioning, second bathrooms, and private garage parking. To save further costs, no marketing or real estate agents were used in selling the units. In order to promote owner-occupiers and discourage speculators, Nightingale Housing deploys restrictive legal agreements on built units, limiting profits on resale for a set time period.

Designing for greater benefit and reduced profit comes with challenges. The financial crisis of 2008 required The Commons to deviate from its intended financial structure by enlisting the help of an ethical developer. Other projects in the pipeline have seen objections over the lack of parking because, even though car sharing options and public transport are nearby, city council's car-focused tradition requires available parking spaces. Financing the construction can be

tricky, as profit margins must meet the bank's requirements. Furthermore, delays with planning applications and appeals, which can happen with any development, generate additional legal and holding costs that must in turn be passed on to purchasers.

As cities continue to grow, responsible development that considers material origins and lifecycles, energy usage and inhabitant behaviour is critical for a circular future. Cities must support progressive urban development that could supplant profit-first, wasteful construction practices; it's time the new becomes the norm.

⊕ Pros
Potential to create more affordable and environmentally sensitive housing.

⊖ Cons
Difficult to compete with speculative developers for land purchases in a strong market, requires greater coordination and faces funding challenges.

⊙ Takeaway
New housing development models have the potential to lower economic and environmental impacts on cities, and some zoning codes may need to be revised.

Brighton Waste House

66 There are emerging national networks that will eventually connect anybody who has surplus or waste material to swap, but until that moment, re-using waste requires a lot of time sourcing material.

— Duncan Baker-Brown

Year started
2013 (started), 2014 (opened)

Type
Teaching space and office

Location
Brighton, UK

Industry
Construction, architecture

Category
Education, commodity broker, building

Founders
Duncan Baker-Brown, BBM Sustainable Design, University of Brighton/Cat Fletcher FEEGLEUK/The Mears Group

Website
arts.brighton.ac.uk/business-and-community/the-house-that-kevin-built

The structure's exterior is clad in used carpet tiles.

Discarded vinyl banners used as a vapour control barrier in construction.

The transition to a circular economy will require an updated skill set to maximize material recovery and resource productivity across many sectors. The cultural shift required for this transformation will take collective action based upon research, education, and best practices. How can the next generation's designers and makers be trained to take on these challenges? The design and construction of the Brighton Waste House explores these notions, putting students to task as an educational facility built on the central campus of the University of Brighton.

The Waste House was born out of a novel idea: to create a fully permitted, permanent building from construction waste. With approximately 20% of construction materials wasted in the UK, the Waste House sought to build from these overlooked resources. Ultimately, construction incorporated discarded materials of all kinds, including denim jeans, VHS tapes and toothbrushes. The finished building serves as a classroom, meeting hall and living laboratory. As an exploration of building with scraps and rubbish, the Waste House is commendable, but the pedagogical methods surrounding its construction are equally relevant to the discussion of circularity. The design and construction included students from both the University of Brighton's architecture

57

VHS cassettes repurposed as cavity insulation.

programme and those studying construction nearby at City College Brighton & Hove vocational school. Over 360 students worked together to construct the building and solve some of the most pressing issues as they developed.

When designing with waste, materials can become available at very short notice. As a result, portions of the building must be designed on the fly, sometimes without precedent. The exterior of the building is clad in some 2,000 old office carpet tiles, a material that only became available two months before completion. The corner detail of the unorthodox cladding was an invention of a fifteen-year-old carpentry

student. Being a new material application, the tiles had to be fire tested on site to meet fire safety regulations. Storage of diverse building supplies also proved a challenge. With typical construction, building material is sourced from suppliers and delivered when needed. With the Waste House, the building and design team acted as a commodity broker and kept material on site, fortunately having the city council's approval to use a neighbouring building for ongoing material storage.

Today, the Brighton Waste House stands monument to how we can challenge our perceptions of waste and education. Through the hands-on engagement

Students on
the job site.

of students, untapped assets can
be discovered and repurposed with
imagination and ingenuity, inspiring this
generation and those to come to better
identify and manage valuable, overlooked
resources. Education is paramount in the
societal shift required to make circular
cities a reality.

(+) Pros
Repurposing materials and
providing hands-on training.

(−) Cons
Design and construction process
is more challenging, and results
must be monitored.

(→) Takeaway
Education, research and
experimentation are key in moving
forward, and supporting the
integration of a missing supply
chain network (commodity brokers)
in cities.

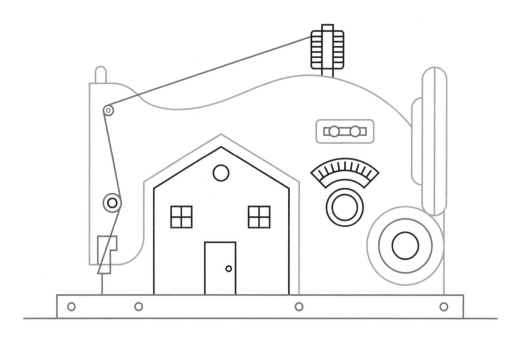

The Empowerment Plan

66 The most important thing to us is that people have secure employment. We are growing at a fast pace, but it is manageable and comfortable.

— Cassie Coravos
Communications & Projects Manager

Year started
2012

Type
Non-profit social enterprise

Location
Detroit, Michigan, USA

Industry
Manufacturing

Category
Reuse, community development, employment, skills training

Founder
Veronika Scott

Website
empowermentplan.org

Inside the
manufacturing facility.

The Empowerment
Plan team.

Current manufacturing practices often put profit margins first, sourcing materials and labour worldwide with little consideration for the social and environmental consequences of their global reach. Can the manufacturing sector be transformed to meet a triple bottom line that provides economic, environmental and societal benefits for those involved? The Empowerment Plan is a move in this direction, challenging the status quo of modern manufacturing, much to the benefit of their employees.

Aiming to break the cycle of poverty through a reimagined manufacturing process, The Empowerment Plan hires and trains individuals living in homeless shelters as seamstresses to make coats that transform into sleeping bags, which are distributed to those in need across the USA and Canada. What started as a university class project is now a successful non-profit, having employed nearly forty formerly homeless individuals and producing and distributing over 5,000 coats per year.

The business concept originated when founder Veronika Scott visited shelters in an effort to determine what was needed. She quickly concluded that coats were not a solution for homelessness and systemic poverty; jobs were needed. Taking this to heart, The Empowerment Plan focuses on creating and maintaining jobs for

63

⌃ Seamstresses are trained
to use the sewing machines.

those most in need. The state of Michigan has a long history of manufacturing, and The Empowerment Plan found local companies willing to help. The clothing company Carhartt donated the first sewing machines and supplies. Currently, General Motors donates material for the lining of the coats, made from upcycled automotive door insulation. In addition, The Empowerment Plan connects their employees to a wide range of social services to help them make the transition back to a more stable existence, including educational programmes, housing assistance, and financial literacy classes. Job security is highly valued within the company. They are careful to expand operations in a responsible way, unwilling

to jeopardize their employees' newly gained stability. In the coming years, they hope to move to a larger facility in Detroit, open a new manufacturing location in a nearby city, and begin production of a coat for consumers.

In spite of a long decline of manufacturing in the USA, The Empowerment Plan has managed to transform the lives of some of the most vulnerable and marginalized through training and engagement. Their manufacturing model focuses on people instead of profit, bettering the community as they invest in social capital. New business models have the potential to advance the human condition without

Coats that transform into sleeping bags are
produced and distributed to those in need.

sacrificing the natural world that we
depend upon.

⊕ Pros
Employees valued in
manufacturing process.

⊖ Cons
Reliant on donations to make it work.

→ Takeaway
Manufacturing can be rethought
to not be solely driven by profit.

Fintry Development Trust

66 We developed a sort of smart grid project, where we can take local renewable electricity and see how we can best use that within the community.

— Matthew Black
Community Project Manager

Year started
2007

Type
Company and charity

Location
Fintry, Scotland, UK

Industry
Energy

Category
Renewable energy, co-ownership, technology

Founders
Fintry Renewable Energy Enterprise (FREE)

Website
fintrydt.org.uk

Matthew Black of Fintry Development
Trust with a new solar panel.

As cities strive to become more self-sufficient with the creation of renewable energy production, there is an opportunity to reconfigure the traditional relationships between energy suppliers and municipalities. Instead of an energy conglomerate cornering the local energy market, citizens can develop their own energy futures, spreading the financial, social and environmental benefits across their community. In rural Scotland, Fintry Development Trust is an example, reaping the rewards of community-driven, local energy production.

Fintry Development Trust grew from Fintry Renewable Energy Enterprise (FREE), which was developed after a wind farm developer approached the community for support of a proposed project nearby. A joint venture with the developer was negotiated. Instead of 14 wind turbines, 15 would be built. The village of Fintry would pay for the capital costs of the additional turbine, while earning a percentage of the wind farm's income. FREE took out a loan to finance this investment on behalf of the community, marking the first time a village in the UK entered into a joint venture agreement with a renewable energy developer.

In the years since the wind turbine project was completed, the Development Trust continued to build community-

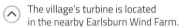
The village's turbine is located
in the nearby Earlsburn Wind Farm.

A look down Main Street
in the village of Fintry.

oriented, energy-producing installations. A biomass-fuelled heating scheme was constructed to serve around 25 households in the village, providing much needed affordable heating, while another installation using geothermal, ground-sourced heat pumps is in development. In addition, a smart grid project was established, allowing local renewable electricity to be distributed within the community. Fintry Development Trust also offers home consultations to locals in further efforts to improve energy efficiency.

Although the 'Fintry Model' of community co-investment does have its origins in a rural community of 700 people, there are shared characteristics with urban neighbourhoods. The scale of projects could be replicable in small city districts, allowing neighbours to better control their own energy production and distribution. Many urban areas also share issues of energy poverty, having households that are not able to adequately heat their homes in an affordable manner. Increased citizen engagement in these issues could lead to more localized solutions and cleaner energy production.

Community inclusion and ownership of the wind turbine was a catalyst for the development of renewable energy technologies in Fintry. Its development also spurred the financing and implementation of additional citizen-based projects, making Fintry a leader of community implemented renewable energy projects. Other cities can follow suit, stimulating the creation a circular future that empowers the lives of residents.

(+) Pros
Generates power and income locally and increases self-reliance in the community.

(−) Cons
Requires local investment, which is not risk-free.

(→) Takeaway
Communities can benefit from co-owning smart and sustainable technologies.

Vandebron

66 Let's hope there are other markets where there is also a lack of transparency, like in food, medicine or clothing, where our model will be copied and pasted.

— Chiel van Leeuwen
Business Development

Year started
2014

Type
For-profit social enterprise

Location
Amsterdam, the Netherlands

Industry
Energy, utilities

Category
Renewable energy, peer-to-peer

Founders
Remco Wilcke, Matthijs Guichelaar and Aart van Veller

Website
vandebron.nl

Energy producers Bernard & Karin Kadijk can sell the energy they produce directly to consumers.

Cities can work toward energy independence with a threefold strategy: by using less energy, by self-producing renewables, and by selling the surplus of their own renewable energy production. Unfortunately, the business model of traditional energy companies does not encourage these innovations. Vandebron is a Dutch energy start-up company, founded to bring transparency to the energy marketplace while creating a peer-to-peer model for green energy transactions. In 2014, 63% of households in the Netherlands thought they were buying green energy, but in fact it was closer to 5%. This could be tied to the fact that, through 'greenwashing', energy companies are able to purchase certificates for their grey energy from foreign energy suppliers. With the adaption of a clever business model, Vandebron is able to pursue their goals while encouraging truly cleaner energy consumption and production.

As an independent service provider, Vandebron does not produce energy; they facilitate the transaction between the energy producer and consumer on their online marketplace. Unlike a traditional energy company that makes profit by purchasing cheap energy and selling it at a higher price in maximum volumes, Vandebron earns income with a fixed monthly fee. While consumers don't have the ability to control the source of every kilowatt-hour of electricity flowing through their homes, they can decide how the energy they buy is sourced and delivered to the grid. Currently, over one hundred independent energy producers supply over 100,000 customers with 100% sustainable and locally sourced electricity. Getting this energy for a better price compared to using other energy suppliers also encourages producers to invest even more in sustainable energy production.

(∧) Ab Aaldering in front
of his solar array.

With a growing consumer base, one obstacle facing Vandebron is a possible shortage of green energy to distribute. Rather than entering the energy production arena, which would create a market bias, Vandebron aims to incentivize new energy investments by increasing consumer demand. They are also focusing on campaigning for energy consciousness. With reduced energy consumption, more connections can be made within their green energy network, in turn reducing demand for fossil fuel-based energy production.

Through the creative integration of their core values into their business plan, Vandebron has created a sustainable and successful social enterprise. In two and a half years they have grown from a staff of four to over one hundred, and have effectively disrupted an antiquated industry. Their business model could be applied to other industries that lack transparency and are dominated by established giants upholding a model designed for maximum financial gains. It is possible to ingrain social and environmental values into large-scale business enterprises, and it should be a hallmark of business as usual in the fast-approaching future.

Closed Loop Fund

66 We are evolving our platform to be a solution provider for the circular economy; an investor to really build that bridge to circularity.

— Rob Kaplan
Closed Loop Fund

Year started
2014

Type
For-profit hybrid social enterprise and social impact fund

Location
New York, NY, USA

Industry
Recycling, finance

Category
Reuse, waste, corporations, investment

Founders
Walmart and others

Website
closedlooppartners.com

Lakeshore Recycling Systems' Heartland Recycling Center sorts, separates and allocates over 20 tons of waste per hour.

Inside the QRS plastic recovery system in Baltimore, MD.

Diverting materials to landfills is a costly and wasteful activity for cities. Municipalities and businesses in the USA spent more than $5 billion to dispose of waste in 2015 alone. With less than 35% of waste materials recycled or composted in the USA, a large portion of commodities that could be reused are discarded, which is a missed economic and environmental opportunity. A major barrier to increasing recycling rates is the significant investment required to collect, sort, and process unwanted materials. The Closed Loop Fund was created by a group of large brand owners and retailers united to help solve this problem.

As an investment platform, The Closed Loop Fund provides below market rate loans to create or improve municipal and private recycling facilities across the USA, with long-term goals of proving both the environmental and financial returns of recycling. The initiative's corporate investors are aware that their supply chains would benefit with increased access to more recycled material. With plans to invest $100 million by 2020, they are also aware that more infrastructure is required to divert materials from waste flows into recycling and manufacturing streams. To date, ten projects across the USA have been carried out thanks to $20 million from the fund, and leveraging an additional $60 million from other

investors. These projects have helped cities save money and reduce waste by diverting materials from landfills and generating revenue from the sale of the rescued commodities.

The Closed Loop Fund hopes to serve as a model for additional investment in recycling infrastructure. As an open-source organization, they are focused on sharing data and information, including best practices, waste diversion results and financial returns. They believe that their investment-based model could be well-suited for emerging markets in developing countries, transportation projects and for other enterprises with large upfront capital costs. Proving that this innovative investment approach works is crucial for its expanded application in the recycling sector and beyond.

With the establishment of this investment fund, large corporations have proven that they are interested in a more circular material future and are willing to help finance the infrastructural projects that are required to make it a reality. Collective action is creating facilities that are needed yet difficult to implement independently. By revealing the economic opportunities in our culture of waste, advancements can be made in creating closed-loop material systems.

 Waste Commission of Scott County's new
"Go All In" curbside collection program.

⊕ Pros
Large amounts of investment
capital are generated for
infrastructural redesign.

⊖ Cons
Relies on large corporations
for funding.

→ Takeaway
The will (and incentive) to
approach circularity exists
at the corporate level.

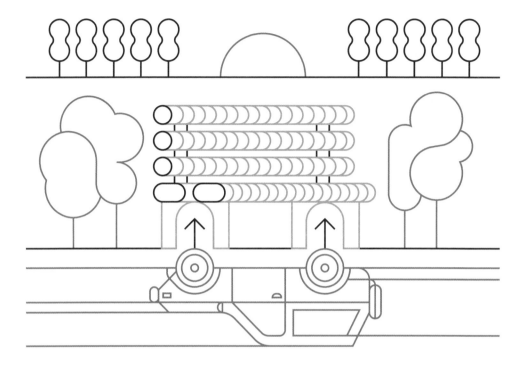

United States Business Council for Sustainable Development

66 We're working in tandem with governments and companies to achieve common goals on materials. Public-private collaboration will open new doors to achieve greater resource efficiency while creating economic, environmental, and societal benefits.

– Andrew Mangan

Year started
1992

Type
Non-profit

Location
Austin, Texas, USA

Industry
Waste management

Category
Resource management, commercial waste, material exchange

Founder
Andrew Mangan

Website
usbcsd.org

A project meeting discussing reuse opportunities.

Consumer waste habits are relatively visible within the city, but citizen's waste only accounts for a small portion of total refuse disposed. In the UK, for example, when measured by weight, commercial waste totals more than twice than that of residential garbage. If closed material loops are to be achieved, cities must be conscious of the waste management practices in commercial and manufacturing sectors. Acting as a materials matchmaker for over twenty years, the United States Business Council for Sustainable Development (US BCSD) works at metropolitan, state and national scales to connect the waste streams of various companies.

As a collaboration platform, the US BCSD helps businesses and organizations of all kinds identify material re-use opportunities by setting up Materials Marketplace projects in cities and regions. When developing a new network of exchange, the US BCSD galvanizes the support from a minimum of 30–40 businesses within the region. In confidence, they collect available and wanted materials information from each participant. Working with a diverse team of support that can include policy makers, government agencies, academia and other non-profit organizations, the US BCSD works to identify and implement materials reuse opportunities based on the Highest and Best Use (HBU) principle.

Material exchange programmes differ depending on location. In Detroit, large-scale manufacturers such as General Motors (GM) are coordinating material streams with other industries. In Austin, Texas, where large-scale manufacturing is less common, service industry and small-scale businesses tend to trade in business furniture and organic and packaging materials more frequently. Since its 2014 start in Austin, over 200 participants have completed more than 170 transactions using the platform. As the US BCSD's Materials Marketplace grows, activities are increasingly large in scale.

Materials Marketplace launched as a pilot programme in 2015, working with large companies on a national scale. During the summer of 2015, 23 companies with 78 facilities made 2.4 million tons of material available for exchange. The financial benefits of material diversion become more obvious at a large scale. GM has generated close to $1 billion in annual revenue through recycling and reuse of its 'waste'. The beneficial reuse of materials can reduce operational costs and environmental footprints, while spurring local economic development.

Material exchange is a vital component of the circular economy. Reuse and repurposing minimizes production with virgin materials and diverts material streams away from landfills. With

 Spent grain from breweries is an abundant material that can be used for food products or animal feed.

systemic changes in progress, companies and municipalities should fully embrace a culture of material collaboration for a more economically and environmentally prosperous future.

⊕ Pros
Manages material exchange for companies, reducing waste and creating opportunity.

⊖ Cons
Requires a level of commitment and transparency from companies.

⊘ Takeaway
Collaboration platforms and services are essential to a circular future.

Conclusion

These 16 cases represent ventures, networks and purpose-driven operational experiments. While many are bound by context, all contain seeds to initiate new approaches, and all shed light on the complex reality of transitioning from a linear to a circular system. Although a necessary transition, it is difficult to overturn an impalpable system that steers our behaviours to support it every day. Yet when we take conscious action to create change, we can and we will see a new circular city unveiling in front of our eyes. The cases analysed here show that things can be done differently, and doing so can create incalculable benefits. In these concluding remarks, we summarize the most important lessons learned from those working on the front lines of circular change, with the aim to bring their needs and ambitions to a wider arena in the following chapters.

From small-scale attempts such as stichting Biomeiler, Solidarity Fridge, Brooklyn Microgrid and WASTED, we learned that the hyper-local is a new field of action with increased impact potential. These examples help us understand that the community of users is itself paramount in initiating a change. Understanding the needs of this community is necessary to set a path of action, where actors who provide resources, knowledge, material, ideas and solutions negotiate unwritten social contracts. At the hyper-local scale, people are there to be listened to, communities can be a trigger for change, or can implement change on its own; for example, by changing habits or being rewarded for choosing to change behaviour. Problems with the hyper-local scale are that every attempt is quite dependent on the goodwill of the community and larger systems can hinder their impact. The issue of scale is one of the biggest limitations of the development of the circular city. Where do we find enough resources to support the needs of this whole global-local population? Hyper-locality is a solution only for some circular development fields, and some communities are more prone to change in one field than in another. Yet what we find is that ultimately, starting from these communities can be a highly intelligent strategy to initiate a circular revolution, even if very small.

In other cases, we dig deep into a new layer of action, seemingly integrated within a local community of users. Here, we look briefly at the street level, zooming in on the retail revolution and housing and food waste. With LENA the fashion library, Library of Things, Toronto Tool Library, Instock, Plant Chicago and Nightingale Housing, we surfed one of the waves composing an ocean of new circular business concepts sprinkled throughout western cities. These cases present new retail concepts based on shared ownership, vertical integration of shared services and resource optimization. These lead us to claim that, while closing material loops is of the utmost importance, fruitful alternatives to ownership is one of the most essential focal points of turning citizens into agents of circular change. It is widely echoed that 'product cycle design' or 'designing for circularity' are the most important and crucial strategies to undertake in order to transform our lives into circular ones. However, while necessary, these are long, complicated processes that imply operational changes and regulatory revolutions. Looking at these cases, we see that the street level represents a space for immediate, agile action. Retailers and inspired social entrepreneurs are working to change the way goods and services are consumed, supplied, reused and valued. Traditional brands both fear and appreciate this approach: some look at this new economy as the death of mass consumerism, while others see opportunities for new business models. We see the opportunities in widespread subscriptions to less and more robust, better-built products and services. This affects the life in cities also from a social and political perspective—shared ownership implies the development of a series of interactions that have not yet been defined, regulated, or in some instances, imagined. If we learned that communities are willing to take part in circular change at the small-scale, we now understand that this change can support the creation of a series of new urban services, which consequently require new rules and regulations. The challenge is to both anticipate and react with insight as we set new standards. Moving to a larger scale, the last cases we considered provide a far wider vision of the circular city, leading into the following chapters.

With Brighton Waste House, The Empowerment Plan, Fintry Development Trust, Vandebron, The Closed Loop Fund and the US Council for Sustainable Development, we looked at a select group of established endeavours that are making a difference in terms of quantitative achievements and creating impact by empowering extensive communities. The Brighton Waste House provides a clear, stimulating and inspirational method to bring circularity into the next generations of builders. It is widely claimed that education is a very effective strategy to implement more predominant circular cities. Brighton Waste House highlights that educational processes are critical to transitioning to circularity. Education coincides with empowerment. The Empowerment Plan shows how education and empowerment can drive new business approaches where circularity (reuse of automotive and clothing industry by-products) is a means to address issues like homelessness to achieve a more equal city. Focused on energy, Fintry Development Trust and Vandebron empower citizens by providing positive, alternative strategies that address resource exploitation. How they allocate circular resources to their members offers great inspiration if looked at on a wider scale. Imagine having a service that allows citizens to choose local, sustainably supplied necessities such as energy and water, or general materials needed for everyday life. Much like The Closed Loop Fund or the US Council for Sustainable Development, these cases represent new commodity brokers: an emerging service area needed to provide and manage the right resources to enable circular cycles to flourish. In these conditions, circular city making leads towards stability and balance, leaving the path of excessive growth. Optimization is based on a shared need to connect communities, industries and regulatory bodies. In this chapter, we learn that this process does not only focus on by-product exchange, but also on education, regulation and empowerment of urban agents. In the following chapters, we look into attempts that take this varied juxtaposition of best practices and compile it into local policy.

———

References

Baker-Brown, Duncan. Personal interview. 17 Oct. 2016.

Black, Matthew. Personal interview. 02 Nov. 2016.

Coravos, Cassie. Personal interview. 21 Oct. 2016.

Crespo Gadea, Ainhoa. Personal interview. 12 Nov. 2016. (confirm name order)

Dyment, Ryan. Personal interview. 29 Nov. 2016.

He, Rui. Personal interview. 04 Nov. 2016.

Jansen, Elisa. Personal interview. 05 Oct. 2016.

Kaplan, Rob. Personal interview. 09 Nov. 2016.

Kessler, Scott. Personal interview. 02 Dec. 2016.

Nightingale Housing. Questionnaire. 07 Nov. 2016.

Pereira, Jonathan. Personal interview. 08 Nov. 2016.

Scholtens, Frank. Personal interview. 07 Oct. 2016.

Seddik, Selma. Personal interview. 21 Oct. 2016.

van Leeuwen, Chiel. Personal interview. 14 Nov. 2016.

Wyatt, Sophia. Personal interview. 09 Nov. 2016.

Circular City:
A Selection of
Policy Approaches

Marijana Novak
CITIES Foundation

Introduction

An *Array of Circular Endeavours* showed approaches to circularity initiated by people within cities. This chapter asks what the city can do, diving in at the urban and regional level to learn how municipalities are supporting and can elevate circular urban harmony. Cities have a unique position. They can leverage between neighbourhoods and national frameworks by connecting hyper-local and national networks, which creates opportunity to engage with industry. They can also link governments to the private sector, and monitor and incentivize civil society.

Circularity encompasses many notions. To name a handful: a holistic view of consumption and production, an enhanced sense of responsibility for the environment, a more elegant system design, a tool for political resilience. At the same time, our cities are each so different. Approaches to circularity must be carefully designed, tailored to meet cultural and contextual landscapes. We want optimal system transitions that create the right environment for self-organization, yet the interconnectedness of cities makes catering for the different priorities and incentives of citizens and enterprises highly complex.

This chapter presents four approaches to circularity, zooming in on Seoul, South Korea; Flanders, Belgium; Rotterdam, the Netherlands; and Ljubljana, Slovenia. These examples are chosen to represent variation in how and at what levels cities are engaging with circularity. By looking at strategies and processes employed at the municipal and regional level, this chapter puts forth the inherent complexity, but also the utility and possibilities of employing circular city approaches in urban development.

The modern commute indicates the contrast
of digital connection vs. social isolation.

Seoul: Sharing City
Infrastructure and Support
for a 'Sharing Economy'
to Optimize Resource Use

^ Three young girls investigate the particulars
of a house share they might participate in.

The city of Seoul, South Korea, officially embraced the concept of the sharing economy in 2012 and remains the largest municipally led example of such an endorsement. Seoul is a global leader in both commercial success and connective capacity, with flourishing business and technological industries and well-integrated, advanced infrastructure. It is one of the densest cities in the world and hosts a high-tech, fast-paced culture: the consumption level of the citizens is taking the city beyond its limits. In an age when urbanization is so intensely scrutinized, Seoul embodies key elements that make it a prime example for investigation.

Parallelling these technological and economic advancements is a familiar, raw urban underside of inequality and increasing waste management issues. The bustling city measures a heightened sense of isolation, anonymity, and even depression among its citizens, as the older cultural sense of 'jeong' (community) is seen to be slipping away, or to have already vanished in this post-modern urban metropolis.

Sharing City Seoul is an initiative launched in response to these very issues. Led by mayor Park Won-Soo, who served as a human rights activist for thirty years, the project has three publicized objectives relating to the popular trinity of profit, planet, and people: the aim is to stimulate local economies through encouraging the recycling of 'resources', and in turn, to create a healthy community of interconnected networks.

———

Policy-making on Taking and Wasting

Sharing City Seoul started with the development of five key policies designed to promote the uptake of sharing initiatives by citizens and organizations, as well as the development of support systems for sharing schemes at multiple levels.

The definition of sharing, in this case, stems from two policies. The first is sufficiently broad to encompass the notion of creating all and any type of value via the joint use of resources, where resources include abstract offerings such as talent and experience. The second deals with how the city qualifies participating bodies as sharing, including the criteria they must meet to register on the city's online database of local sharing services. These two policies are useful in combination because they offer validation of offered sharing services while sifting out and promoting leading practices. Leniency inherent in these two policies is useful at an early stage of implementation, but they should become more demanding over time as regulation and support continue to evolve.

On that note, a third policy pays special attention to the improvement of laws and institutions relevant to strengthening a legitimate sharing economy. For example, privately run taxi services such as Uber were banned in Seoul just this year (2016), while the technology was harnessed to create an application supporting local taxi services. This contrasts with what happens in other cities, such as San Francisco, where extensive sharing services tend to create tension, rather than resolve it, via apps and services that dip and dive around legislation.

The fourth policy incentivizes local administrative participation through predefined city districts, known as 'Gus'. Scored on their effectiveness in promoting designated projects, districts are offered the potential for extra budget based on the extent of their success. Fifth and finally, the city itself has made its 'assets' available to citizens. Buildings and otherwise unused spaces are available for meetings and citizen-led initiatives. Documents such as expense reports, public data and other city or district office data are also available online and can be downloaded. Despite this policy, there is still no information available as to the impact delivered within districts, or any clear qualitative and quantitative metrics of success.

Tangible Outcomes and Connection to People

Since Sharing City Seoul's start in 2012, countless programmes have been implemented to spread awareness about a sharing culture. Hundreds of apps and businesses have been launched, and the city professes to have saved significant amounts of money and considerably reduced waste. Granted the tangled complexity of an emerging sharing economy, concrete figures for analysis remain unavailable. Of the diverse multitude of apps and start-ups blooming out of the sharing efforts, some have been more successful than others. For example, car sharing and libraries for children's clothes have been readily taken up across the city, while other services such as tool libraries were less successful.

An online network, sharehub.kr, lends particular aid to the collaborative consumption system by providing an open directory of sharing services and projects around the city. In recognition of the internet as an engine powering the sharing movement, the city established some two thousand new wireless access points in markets, parks and government offices, making Seoul the world's most 'connected city'.

Despite the city's general wealth and 'connected' status, only 60% of citizens have access to smartphones. Counter to intuition, this makes the sharing initiative relatively exclusive. But not worthless: in terms of countering excessive resource use, those with smartphones may be the prime perpetrators of consumptive waste, and therefore the prime target for impactful behavioural shifts. Just think of the impact if the 60% of smartphone users adopted sharing practices. This, however, is an unlikely outcome, and surveys indicate that programme awareness levels vary all the way from 1 in 10 to 1 in 2. With no real knowledge of the extent and depth of the programme's uptake, we can deduce that Sharing City Seoul certainly has room for growth, yet has also stirred a tangible shift in awareness action toward sharing.

―――

Conclusion

Collaborative consumption and the sharing economy in Seoul have been met with mixed reviews. On the one hand, it brings positive results associated directly with the initiative's key goals. On the other hand, it is associated with a heightened sense of commodification in citizens' lives and the rise of sharing monopolies. At city government level, greater regulatory involvement could both curb and harness the associated negatives towards the greater good.

The city describes the programme's adoption as 'slow', expressing little concern in this regard, instead emphasizing their efforts to expand sharing city initiatives, including wider education and marketing programmes. Part of this effort involves financing

The high-tech, fast-paced environment
can squeeze citizens to the sideline.

particularly successful 'sharing businesses', as well as providing customized consulting
and promotional help so these companies can upscale in the international sharing
marketplace. Focusing on strong companies is a good approach, however the extra
effort to go international seems out of line with the initiative's localized aims.

Institutionalizing change at such a scale requires high-level adjustments coupled with
small, targeted efforts in a constant cycle of adjustment and adaptation. Seoul is a
tangible example of how a city can put significant effort into the infrastructure of an
idea, but regulatory effort must support it for outcomes to manifest and really spur
a shift in mindset at the individual level.

92

References

Hong, Emily. "Lessons from Seoul's Two Sharing Economies." *Tech Crunch*, 14 Aug. 2015, www.techcrunch.com/2015/08/14/lessons-from-seouls-two-sharing-economies/. Accessed 17 Jan. 2017.

Johnson, Cat. "Is Seoul the next Great Sharing City?" *Our World*. United Nations University, 05 Aug. 2013, www.ourworld.unu.edu/en/is-seoul-the-next-great-sharing-city. Accessed 17 Jan. 2017.

Johnson, Cat. "Despite Slow Adoption, Seoul Doubles Down On Sharing City Project." *Shareable*, 29 Oct. 2015, www.shareable.net/blog/despite-slow-adoption-seoul-doubles-down-on-sharing-city-project. Accessed 17 Jan. 2017.

Johnson, Cat. "Sharing City Seoul: a Model for the World." *Shareable*, 03 June 2014, www.shareable.net/blog/sharing-city-seoul-a-model-for-the-world. Accessed 17 Jan. 2017.

Kang, Junhee, Keeyeon Hwang, and Sungjin Park. "Finding Factors that Influence Carsharing Usage: Case Study in Seoul." Sustainability 8.8 (2016): 709.

Lamshed, Bella. "Cities of tomorrow: How this city regained its Seoul." 09 Feb. 2016, *1 Million Women*, www.1millionwomen.com.au/blog/cities-tomorrow-how-city-regained-its-seoul. Accessed 17 Jan. 2017.

McLaren, Duncan, and Julian Agyeman. *Sharing Cities: A Case for Truly Smart and Sustainable Cities*. MIT Press, 2015.

Orsi, Janelle, et al. "Policies for Shareable Cities: A sharing economy policy primer for urban leaders." Shareable and the Sustainable Economies Law Center (2013).

Share Hub. http://english.sharehub.kr. Accessed 17 Jan. 2017.

"Seoul, ready to share with the world! Seoul e-Government" Seoul Metropolitan Government, http://citynet-ap.org/wp-content/uploads/2014/06/Seoul-e-Government-English.pdf. Accessed 17 Jan. 2017.

"'The Sharing City, Seoul' Project." Metropolis, www.metropolis.org/awards/5th-edition-2014/sharing-city-seoul-project. Accessed 17 Jan. 2017.

While still the busiest port in Europe, Rotterdam
is moving beyond its industrial heritage.

Rotterdam: CityLab010
A Finance and Support
Mechanism for Hyper-local
Circularity

The City of Rotterdam is building its future from the ground up, and their CityLab010 initiative is the foundation. With a total of €3 million in funding made available to citizens and small businesses with ideas for a more sustainable Rotterdam, projects can be pitched on the CityLab010 website. Judged on their level of innovation, capacity to succeed and 'social relevance', successful projects are provided with a grant and additional services from the city to aid business acceleration, collaboration between industries and other support functions.

CityLab010 focuses on promoting citizen engagement rather than on measuring or mapping final results, and provides opportunities for ideas that do not necessarily fit directly into 'policy' directives. Both of these characteristics indicate the project's inherent innovation and forward-thinking approach, most notable in the funding scheme and process of cross-collaboration between municipality, citizens and other relevant local experts.

Overall, the project inspires and fosters civil engagement by encouraging and enabling citizens to gain ownership over urban processes that are important to them. This environment assists in the 'on-the-ground' implementation of the circular economy, and in shifting the general consumer/citizen mindset toward a sense of responsibility for the surrounding built and natural environment, for the 'commons'.

———

Make the Circle Bigger: Round Two

CityLab010's funding and support began in 2015. Projects were described as fitting within one of nine broad categories that each contribute to the city's positive development. Out of approximately 150 submissions in the first year, 46 projects were approved across the nine categories. Funding amounts range from as little as €5,000 all the way to €150,000, depending on a project's scope and application.

The broad range of funding facilitates diverse project submissions. Some are more business-oriented than others. For example, BroodNodig was funded to valorize bread waste and create biogas; The idea of 'Meer (schone) lucht' to tackle air pollution by strategically placing air pumps for motor vehicles (as low tire pressure produces greater emissions); and community garden Voedseltuin to occupy previously undeveloped land and promote a sense of community, while offering the benefits of locally grown products. Continuing in 2016, CityLab010 has racked up some 200 submissions over two funding rounds. The second round saw a similarly diverse range of projects, however the 'winners' are yet to be announced.

The project is relatively new, leaving little time to generate sufficient analytical information. As a consequence, the number of projects that might be funded is

⌃ Rotterdam is working to improve environmental conditions throughout the city, especially air quality. The 'milieuzone' is a demarcated area in the city that only allows vehicles meeting certain emission standards.

not clear, nor the details of already funded projects—how many are still actively supported, how many still exist, and how many are now self-sustaining? In sum, there is not enough information to make a qualitative or quantitative assessment as to the project's real success at this stage, which touches on the difficulty of clearly tracking the progress of such complex, innovative initiatives.

Networks over Nodes

CityLab010 aims to connect citizens and provide a means to build an established network of innovation and expertise in the city. It is not easy to solve urban social problems, and recognizing this, the project calls for a different approach: let the people

'Meer (schone) lucht', a CityLab 010 initiative, helps vehicle owners maintain proper tire pressure (to reduce emissions) by installing solar powered air pumps throughout the city.

of Rotterdam decide what is important to them and let them tackle the problems themselves.

Anyone legally registered in the City of Rotterdam, or in the Netherlands for that matter, can apply for a grant—so long as the project fits within one of the nine themes. The amount of funding allocated to each theme reveals the city's priorities: Education in first position and Sustainability and Mobility in fourth. This method allows the municipality's strategic funding allocation to organically align with citizens' needs. Funding amounts per theme can be adjusted going forward, should the demand be significantly out of line with supply.

Typically, successful projects are quite small and target a specific customer base or city area. In turn, successes can lead to budding nodes of activity that spread demand and awareness, while citizens gain an increasing sense of ownership and capacity to control chosen aspects of their city. Ideally, supporting this decentralized proliferation of projects could lead to a more socially responsible and sustainable Rotterdam. With that hope, CityLab010 provides business support, supply chain advice and collaboration services to selected projects.

––––

Conclusion

CityLab010 connects local citizens to municipal means in an effort to collaboratively solve a wide range of problems in a mutually beneficial manner. It does form a strong base for strategic development; however, by design the initiative selects citizens who already have some feeling for circularity, while not involving those less familiar or concerned—a part of the population that is critical to achieving deep-set change. This raises outreach concerns, which could be countered via the creation of a programme to educate and empower communities that would otherwise not even be aware of initiatives like CityLab010.

While the project has visibly kick-started citizen's interest, engagement and responsibility in the city, it does not address continuity. This is especially pertinent because not all the initiatives are commercially viable, leaving them to whither when funding and public support ends. This possible scenario, however, also pushes citizens who are running funded projects to work harder to make their projects better and stronger by providing more direct value to the city and its citizens. Analysis and study of the ventures could provide insights into where and how regulatory bodies could further support this process of circular evolution.

The networking aspect and small-scale approach strongly relate CityLab010 to circular cities. Establishing knowledge networks and collaborating is crucial for implementing a robust circular economy, and horizontal integration and information transfer is required to create closed loops in supply chains of all sizes across the city. CityLab010 promotes knowledge networks from the ground up, defining a path towards hyper-localized circular city making, and this seems to be an effective method for jump-starting circularity.

———

References

CITYLAB010. www.citylab010.nl. Accessed 17 Jan. 2017.

Erasmus Magazine. www.erasmusmagazine.nl. Accessed 17 Jan. 2017.

Gemeente Rotterdam. www.rotterdam.nl. Accessed 17 Jan. 2017.

Tappan Communicatie. www.tappan.nl. Accessed 17 Jan. 2017.

Twitter. www.twitter.com. Accessed 17 Jan. 2017.

 Multi-stakeholder collaboration in a workshop hosted by Plan C teasing out circularity in the timber supply chain.

Belgium: Flanders' Materials Programme
Knowledge and Practical Support for Trading and Reusing Materials

Plan C supports small recycling programmes such as YUMA, which make 3D-printed glasses from waste materials.

Flanders' Materials Programme (FMP) won The Circulars award in 2016 for a comprehensive, seemingly all-encompassing approach to managing resources across industries in the Flanders region of Belgium.

Flanders is a compact region that heavily exports high-value manufactured goods, which creates a large demand for raw materials—predominantly metals—and generates significant waste streams from its factories. Circular principles therefore serve Flanders well to deal with both supply chain and import risk, as well as the reduction of landfilled waste due to high-value extraction. These two issues were key drivers in the development of Flanders as a recycling and remanufacturing hub over the last few decades, with the Public Waste Agency (OVAM) established in 1983. Since then, bans and taxes on landfilling and incarceration were set and steadily increasing and advanced collection and recycling methodologies were established as waste legislation was continuously developed and implemented.

Essentially, the FMP aims to streamline the many public and private initiatives in the field of sustainable materials management into a coherent whole. Their approach centres on the establishment of a communication network with a 'shared vision' on materials management and a related set of 45 action items. The scope of action extends from the end-of-life phase to the entire materials cycle, examining the impact of design on the waste phase, ways to promote industrial symbiosis, and how the shared use of products can reduce the emissions footprint.

The Past Brings Presence to the Future

Over the last 35 years, in Flanders recycling efforts have increased in response to rising awareness around growing environmental, supply chain and import risks, as well as general regulatory pressure concerning waste management. Policy, research, and practical improvements have developed in parallel. In 2010, the 'circular economy' formally made its way onto Belgium's political agenda, and more specifically, its northern region: Flanders. By then, the long-established Public Waste Agency had amassed experience that could be harnessed into a holistic regional vision. In 2011, circularity was politically prioritized further, as Sustainable Materials Management was listed as one of the thirteen major societal challenges for Flanders. Following in 2012, the FMP was formally developed. Thus, although the FMP is relatively novel in its formation, it relies heavily on a long-standing foundation dedicated to the management and recycling of materials, which is also a key propeller of its success.

The FMP's implementation encountered obstacles that are expected to remain long-term limitations, leading to under-priced risks, and skills shortages for more progressive operations; the latter is a generally shared concern for circular projects. In response, significant grants have been redirected into educational programmes. In fact, a decent proportion of the 45 actions are related to educational efforts that are channelled into marketing and awareness campaigns, as well as internal growth and understanding. While this action is necessary, its effects will take several years to materialize. To help steer the programme smoothly going forward, all stakeholders should continue engaging with the actions.

Aiming to continue with as little new funding as possible, the FMP relies on adjusting current programmes and redirecting grants and subsidies. This should not be viewed as a half-hearted commitment. Flanders intends to overthrow all substandard programmes in hopes of a complete takeover by more deserving and relevant initiatives.

Circularity as Change Management

The FMP connects with individuals via businesses, aiming to provide circular guidance on political and business decisions by creating shared knowledge networks. In particular, this project stands out because its vision and action plans were designed through consultation with policy makers, practitioners and industry experts. The participative process rendered a set of actions that key stakeholders agreed were practical and valuable, while generating a sense of shared responsibility to carry out the actions.

A host of small and medium enterprises (SMEs) in Flanders do business in broad alignment with the FMP. It is impractical to manage this vast portfolio of businesses and ensure their alignment with circular objectives. To counter this, the FMP carefully selects the most innovative companies to act as influencers and leaders in their sector, allowing them to develop an open yet hierarchical information structure flowing from top to bottom. Sharing the same difficulties and regulatory demands, businesses are indirectly encouraged to collaborate where possible.

The FMP openly recognizes the circular economy as an exercise in change management, and in turn, the importance of the individuals involved in a successful transition. Attention to the individual is maintained by focusing on educational programmes that are available to all players in the field, and also work to raise awareness around the plan's benefits regional importance.

———

Conclusion

Flanders has self-marketed its high potential for the transition to circularity, based in large part on the varied assets just described. The FMP offers an impressive regional plan on how to leverage and arrange those assets to achieve circular goals. Essentially, the region views circularity as an exercise in change management, and policies and institutions have responded accordingly, with the construction of educational programmes, participative planning and a connection to industry. This infrastructure will aid a circular transition if it remains active and in place: circularity efforts are not one-off exercises, but rather require a shift in mindset cultivated throughout ongoing dedication to the process.

The FMP approaches the circular city from a regional and material perspective. Both the need to empower and educate local communities and to provide the proper institutional environment to regulate the change are recognized and set in place through a comprehensive strategy. considering our findings in *An Array of Circular*

Much of the Flanders region is rural in character and dependent on raw material imports.

Endeavours, this approach can be seen as one interpretation of the commodity broker service, noted as a necessary step in optimizing circularity.

The FMP's features contrast with the previous examples in this chapter, which focus on hyper-locality and providing support for citizens' initiatives. This evidences that contextualizing in an area's socio-economic composition and cultural attitude are paramount in defining circular city policy.

––––––

References

Ellen MacArthur Foundation. www.ellenmacarthurfoundation.org. Accessed 17 Jan. 2017.

Governments Going Circular – Global Scan Best Practices. Dutch Sustainable Business. www.govsgocircular.com. Accessed 17 Jan. 2017.

Kazmierczyk, Pawel, et al. "More from less: material resource efficiency in Europe; 2015 overview of policies, instruments and targets in 32 countries." (2016).

Langeveld, J.W.A. "Results of the JRC-SCAR Bioeconomy survey" Biomass Research. (2015). https://www.scar-swg-sbgb.eu/lw_resource/datapool/_items/item_24/survey_bioeconomy_report1501_full_text.pdf. Accessed 17 Jan. 2017.

Leefmilieu Brussel. www.leefmilieu.brussels. Accessed 17 Jan. 2017.

OVAM Ecodesign.link. http://www.ecodesignlink.com. Accessed 17 Jan. 2017.

"Press release: The Public Waste Agency of Flanders and the Flanders' Materials Programme win the Circular Economy Award at the World Economic Forum Annual Meeting in Davos." Vlaams Materialenprogramma, www.vlaamsmaterialenprogramma.be/press-release-the-public-waste-agency-of-flanders-and-the-flanders-materials-programme-win-the. Accessed 17 Jan. 2017.

"The Public Waste Agency of Flanders and the Flanders' Materials Programme Win the Circular Economy Award at the World Economic Forum Annual Meeting in Davos." Vito, 20 Jan 2016, https://vito.be/en/news-events/news/the-public-waste-agency-of-flanders-and-the-flanders-materials-programme-win-the-circular-economy-award. Accessed 17 Jan. 2017.

Research Foundation - Flanders (FWO). www.fwo.be. Accessed 17 Jan. 2017.

Verbeeck, Jorn and Jiska Verhulst. "Transition to a circular economy: the Flanders' Materials Programme." Vlaams Materialenprogramma and Plan C. Presentation, 01 June 2015, www.leefmilieu.brussels/sites/default/files/user_files/4.5_territorial_case_flanders_ovam_plan_c_def.pdf. Accessed 17 Jan. 2017.

Zero Waste Europe. www.no-burn.org. Accessed 17 Jan. 2017.

Walkability and access to nature are
important values in Slovenian city planning.

Ljubljana: Green Aims
Prioritizing Empowerment through a Green Relationship with Built and Natural Environments

Slovenia is a small Central European country with a population of just two million. Over 60% of the land is covered with forests and natural vegetation. A fine achievement in a world overrun with deforestation and land use debates, but it did not happen without action. The government of Slovenia decided to prevent environmental degradation and maintain its relationship with the land, and even to enhance it to a restorative and non-destructive state. Wholeheartedly encompassing principles of circular development, the decision extended across Slovenia, affecting policy from reforestation to urban planning and production to manufacturing.

Circular industrial processing is already a priority in Slovenia. Strong recycling practices are already in place for the country's main natural resource, wood, and the steel industry receives 100% of its inputs from well-handled waste streams.

Green Aims, Green City, Green Heart

In 2016, Ljubljana was given the Green City Award. It was also designated one of the ten cities in Ellen MacArthur Foundation's Circular Cities Network, which aims to share knowledge and good practices among and from cities at the forefront of a circular transition. Although the phrase circularity is relatively new and related policies and practices take time to develop, these ten cities foresaw the value of restorative systems and acted before it became as urgent as it is today. Ljubljana is a green city, with a number of green aims related to energy efficiency, nature and biodiversity, sustainable mobility, preservation of natural water, and solid and water waste management.

Sustainable mobility is already well under way, with varied methods employed to improve this aspect of city life. For example, in 2010, the city issued a transport card allowing intermodal transport use within the city. Well-received, the city plans to create 30 more intermodal transfer points. With continued improvement of cycling and pedestrian lanes, private car use has decreased from 57% in 2003 to 19% in 2013. Longer-term plans include establishing high-speed public transfer routes by 2020 and modernizing the railway infrastructure by 2025.

Today, Ljubljana also has world-class water and waste management facilities, with an interlinked sewage system that combines atmospheric, municipal and mixed streams of water and waste. The sewage system is well-managed and regularly monitored using cameras and other technology. Data is regularly collected and collated to understand where improvements can be made on efficiency and to inform future renovations.

Small and safe, 49% of the urban population
travels by foot or bicycle within the city.

Deep Rooted Foundations Taking Form

Citizens are encouraged to access and 'use' their urban environment in non-destructive ways through, for example, electric transportation and pedestrian zones. In addition, waste bins for different waste streams are found throughout the city. Of course, in order for such changes to create an impact, citizens must accept and support the city's efforts. This isn't always the case. Even a pedestrian zone was met with doubt and scepticism when first proposed. City-held participative planning groups revealed that citizens were positive about the change, but concerned about the lack of alternatives and restriction of movement in the area. The city responded by opening up the area to 'green' options, such as electric cars or bicycles, and implementing electric charge zones and a bicycle sharing system. This approach is commendable because it inspires engagement and a sense of ownership in the city.

Ljubljana's residents seem to be catching on to the green city aims and vision, as several hundreds of residents have sent in proposals and ideas for further improvements. Whether or not these are implemented is not as important as what it indicates—the level of citizen commitment and involvement, which can only be acquired over time as a city delivers on its promises. For at least a decade, Ljubljana has offered its citizens ever-greener and more robust utilities and services. In line with the recent changes in the city centre, this offers legitimacy to the municipality's vision.

Formally involving with circular economic efforts, Ljubljana launched the Circular Change platform, which is increasing stakeholder involvement. The platform is largely used to form a link between individuals and businesses, as well as between individuals and the government on issues of circularity. It also offers opportunities to advance the softer skills associated with a circular transition, including education, leadership recognition, research and advisory work. While Circular Change's efforts predominantly focus on the private sector, the changes the city makes to support these smaller scale economic initiatives remain to be seen.

Conclusion

Prioritizing environmental preservation in Ljubljana forms a broad connection with citizens, as they are provided with a functional 'green' environment to live, work and enjoy life. This is important because circularity is occasionally associated with disruption, but at a systemic level within a city, especially with regards to utilities and service provision, it actually leads to more stability—both environmentally and economically.

Swarming crowds and active participation in Green Mobility Awareness Week.

The successful inclusion and participation of citizens in designing the mobility programme indicates the city's openness and dedication to providing sustainable solutions. As a result, Ljubljana saw a growing number of suggestions from citizens and increased engagement with green development. This is a strong starting point for building a network of communication channels and empowerment mechanisms to further advance the city's green aims.

———

References

"2016 – Ljubljana." *European Commision*, http://ec.europa.eu/environment/europeangreencapital/winning-cities/2016-ljubljana/index.html. Accessed 17 Jan. 2017.

Basle, Andreja. "Creating the future of smart cities in Ljubljana." 04 Oct. 2016, Circular Change, www.circularchange.com/creating-future-smart-cities-ljubljana. Accessed 17 Jan. 2017.

Berden, Simona. "LJUBLJANA EUROPEAN GREEN CAPITAL 2016." Ljubljana - European Green Capital 2016 team. Presentation, 2016, http://ec.europa.eu/environment/europeangreencapital/wp-content/uploads/2016/07-2016/building-an-egc-programme.pdf. Accessed 17 Jan. 2017.

"Central waste water treatment plant of Ljubljana." *JP VODOVOD-KANALIZACIJA*, http://www.vo-ka.si/en/about-company/central-treatment-plant-ljubljana. Accessed 17 Jan. 2017.

"Citizens' Dialogue in Ljubljana, Slovenia." *European Commision*, http://
ec.europa.eu/citizens-dialogues/slovenia/ljubljana3/index_en.htm.
Accessed 17 Jan. 2017.

"Implementation and large-scale deployment of bio-diesel and
CNG fleets in Ljubljana." *Civitas*, http://www.civitas.eu/content/
implementation-and-large-scale-deployment-bio-diesel-and-cng-
fleets-ljubljana. Accessed 17 Jan. 2017.

Isabel Munguia Partida, Ana. "Ljubljana – European Green Capital 2016
joined the Circular Cities Network." 02 Nov. 2016, *Circular Change*, http://
www.circularchange.com/ljubljana-european-green-capital-2016-
joined-circular-cities-network. Accessed 17 Jan. 2017.

Isabel Munguia Partida, Ana. "What we can learn from Ljubljana,
Slovenia – 2016 Green Capital of Europe." 30 June 2016, *Circular Change*,
http://www.circularchange.com/can-learn-ljubljana-slovenia-2016-
green-capital-europe. Accessed 17 Jan. 2017.

"Energy Efficiency Aims" *In Your Pocket*, https://www.inyourpocket.com/
ljubljana/Energy-Efficiency-Aims_136320v. Accessed 17 Jan. 2017.

Ljubljana Marsh Nature Park. http://www.ljubljanskobarje.si/?lang=en.
Accessed 17 Jan. 2017.

"Ljubljana Regional Waste Management Centre." *Mestna občina
Ljubljana*, www.greenljubljana.com/funfacts/ljubljana-regional-waste-
management-centre. Accessed 17 Jan. 2017.

Mestna občina Ljubljana. http://www.ljubljana.si/en. Accessed 17 Jan.
2017.

Simon, D. "Rethinking Sustainable Cities." (2016).

Conclusion

In this chapter, three municipalities and one region engaged in circular implementation were briefly described. In summary, we find that each programme is unique in its method and uptake, and that circular approaches translate into a means for problem solving.

Seoul sets out to tackle increasing individual consumption with the sharing economy. It seems that a slow uptake is due to low interest or general awareness among citizens, unsure of the benefits that changing their lifestyles could bring. Sharing Seoul City could see better results from aligning its incentives more closely with those of the citizens in terms of economy and convenience, as well as developing a more comprehensive approach that includes regulation and education.

Rotterdam is providing funding and support to citizens so they can start their own enterprises focused on improving the city. Irrespective of large-scale municipal and industrial projects, CityLab010 reaches citizens directly, fostering both a broad sense of ownership and real ownership of specific projects to better the commons. The leniency in scope works in the short run, however it might affect the longevity and continuity of the project and its aims.

Flanders aims to close its material loops via the establishment of an industry-wide network with a shared vision, marketing circularity as an exercise in change management. One of the FMP's unique aspects is the interdisciplinary, cross-industry participative planning of varied objectives with shared responsibilities. Continued engagement, effort and streamlined actions by members should allow for more complete, sustained success.

Ljubljana is spearheading a shift toward circularity that springs from Slovenia's long-standing, positive relationship with its natural environment. Increased green infrastructure from smart mobility to pedestrian zones and public recycling bins are lessening the city's environmental impact, while breaking down and re-conceptualizing traditional habits. Using the momentum, Ljubljana is working to stimulate greater public engagement to advance its goals and increase trust with its citizens in shared pursuit of a greener city.

In conclusion, the question of creating an environment conducive to change is dependent on local culture and existing frameworks. There is no one solution, no one approach, and there is never a guarantee that circular programmes at the city level, inherently large and complex, will fully realize their desired outcomes. Multiple programmes with varied objectives and target markets are needed for systems as complex and multidimensional as cities.

Bringing together issues highlighted in *An Array of Circular Endeavours* with this chapter allow key features of circular city making to emerge. At a citizen level: education, participation, empowerment and regulatory engagement to protect individuals and support the right values. At an industry level: the creation of organizational structures that give agency to new commodity brokers allow industrial symbiosis. At a municipal level: dedication to circularity through services and procurement.

Moving beyond the city, the following chapter analyses national approaches in the Netherlands and Sweden. These are two countries where circularity principles have become relatively more mainstream, thus demanding wider, and more developed support networks.

The Role of National Government in Circular City Making

Addressing Possibilities and Constraints in Sweden and the Netherlands

Barbara Koole and Anna Hult
CITIES Foundation

Circular urban development reaches beyond city borders. Like many of today's major issues, it is tied in with wider urban and environmental systems. For example, waste in our cities can be rightfully called a 'wicked problem[1]'—highly complex, consisting of many elements, with incomplete data, prone to change and ultimately tough to solve. On one level, circular city making is so 'wicked' because it challenges existing organizational and governmental structures and policies. This is true for both sector divisions between businesses and for the boundaries of traditional constituencies.

The notion of circular cities should encompass a relational view of space, where territorial identifications are of little importance compared to what is paramount: material flows and human activities. In order to redirect these flows and activities onto a more circular path, policies need to work on local, regional and national levels. What can a central, powerful actor like the national government do to play its part? And what has been done by two of the most progressive national governments in the global north with regard to a circular economy?

This chapter focuses on these questions, exploring what the Dutch and Swedish governments are undertaking to further the circular economy and bring to light the possibilities and challenges of working at a national policy level. To gain insight, we interviewed public officials at Swedish and Dutch ministries who work on issues of the circular economy. In Sweden, we interviewed a civil servant—a member of the Swedish Green Party—at the Department of Finance, and in the Netherlands, we spoke with a senior policy coordinator directly involved in circular economy policy at the Ministry of Infrastructure and the Environment. Their respective positions at different ministries have some similarities, but there are also important differences in their approach to circularity and the policies being implemented.

In the Netherlands, in September 2016 a government-wide programme was presented that proposes targets and provides an outline for circular policies for the coming decades. The target is a 50% waste reduction by 2030 and a fully circular economy by 2050[2]. Our Dutch interviewee, whom we will call Dirk, was involved in the coordination and design of both this programme and its predecessor: 'From waste to resource,' and now plays a role in implementing the new strategies. In Sweden, a circular economy is a priority issue for the government, today mainly handled by the Ministry of Environment. A permanent committee that presented a plan in February 2017 focused on tools for steering industry and business towards a bio-based and circular economy. The issues of waste and closing material loops are central in both the Dutch and Swedish general approaches towards a circular economy. Also, the large societal challenges inherent in a circular transition in both interviews were mentioned, emphasizing a required re-think in all sectors in society.

In order to bring a truly circular city closer, coordination between regional, national and international partners is key. But how are the agendas of such different levels actually working together? Using the Dutch context as an example, strategies regarding circular urban development exist on many levels—from the City of Amsterdam's metropole region, to the aforementioned national programme, the EU's Urban Agenda and the UN's Sustainable Development Goals. In addition, Dirk noted that several departments of the national government are simultaneously working on the circular transition. An example of this is the 'City Deal'. Initiated by the Ministry of Internal Affairs, the deal unites eight Dutch municipalities in advancing circular urban development, in alignment with the programmes led by the ministries of Economic Affairs and Infrastructure and the Environment. This challenges all the actors to keep up to date with developments in all department and at all level. While Dirk did note that contact between policy makers from local to international levels of government has increased in recent years, there is still room for improvement. One challenge is streamlining communication and planning to better leverage all possibilities of mutually reinforced action.

One Swedish reform has received much international attention recently. Coming from the Ministry of Finance, it is part of the first strategy the Swedish government has produced that specifically concerns sustainable consumption. Our interviewee in Sweden, whom we will call Elsa, pointed out that within this strategy, information campaigns and education are tools to steer consumer behaviour. This, however, isn't nearly enough. To add support, a new Swedish tax policy set in action in January 2017 lowers taxes for repairing bikes, textiles, shoes and clothes, in combination with a tax relief for repairing home goods, such as refrigerators. The aim is to encourage people to repair their things, instead of throwing them away and buying new ones. Ultimately, this clearly portrays the general circular shift in behaviour that the government supports, and hopefully triggers that shift in citizen's behaviour.

During our conversation with Dirk, we discussed the Swedish tax reduction initiative, and whether or not such a policy would work well in the Netherlands. The development of new rules and regulations is one of five focus points within the government-wide programme on the circular economy. However, the main challenge in implementing a similar policy in the Netherlands would come down to cooperation across departments. Several relevant ministries, for instance the Ministry of Finance, currently do not regard sustainability and circularity as a core task. An underlying challenge to policymaking going forward seems to be how to enable horizontal cooperation, which is necessary and inherent to circular development.

Sweden could pull off the tax relief policy primarily because the Green Party, currently in power and in coalition with the social democrats, holds one of three ministerial positions at the Ministry of Finance. The tax reform is a political product, and since the policy concerns a tax relief for individuals, it is also rather easy to win support for it.

In addition, its cost is low and it does not involve significant sums of money. How the policy will actually work in practice remains to be seen.

Regarding the territorial comments at the beginning of this chapter, it has been observed within academic work on multi-level governance that highly complex, cross-sector and border-crossing issues such as a circular transition often require functional rather than geographical organizational divisions[3]. One form this could take is a new office with a mandate to involve the necessary players for such ambitious challenges, which has been experimented with in other contexts[4].

Finally, when asked about the biggest current challenge in furthering the circular economy, Dirk pointed out that it is difficult to keep track of societal developments and ongoing initiatives. There seems to be a missing bridge between pioneers of the circular economy and the governmental actors involved in stimulating its development. If on the one hand a governmental actor expresses a want to stimulate and nurture innovations, but on the other hand the initiators do not know how to find their way towards new regulations and support, we can conclude that there is a communication flaw to be addressed.

In conclusion, the main insights from our exploratory interviews at the national governmental level reveal that legislative and coordinating power can prove crucial in realizing circular urban development, however this power is currently not living up to its potential. We also found that there are concrete policies to be implemented in order to encourage circular flows of resources, repairing and remaking. But the main challenge in this endeavour is that circularity implies such a cross-sector approach that it challenges existing structures. This calls for the creation of both cross-sector organizations at the national level and cooperative structures among national, regional and local levels.

Based on these insights to the inherently complex road towards circularity, we believe it would be beneficial to create space for diverging ideas and problem definitions. There seems to be an information deficit, both within government and among practitioners and responsible governmental parties. By involving more circular pioneers with first-hand knowledge in policymaking, best practices and important lessons can be learned, collected and acted upon. This should go further than communication, working towards co-creation. In doing so, the national governments, but also international actors such as the EU, have the potential to increase shared learning among different actors. The alignment and mutual reinforcement of actions could then be increased both horizontally and vertically. In this way, the national government can help inspire ambition, rather than just prescribe explicit actions to cities. To conclude, we do not find insufficient knowledge or a lack of political will when it comes to circularity at the national governmental level, but rather a difficulty in involving the right partners and daring to take, sometimes tough, political decisions.

———

Notes

1 As described by Rittel & Webber in their 1973 article, Rittel, H. W., & Webber, M. M. (1973).

2 https://www.government.nl/binaries/government/documents/policy-notes/2016/09/14/a-circular-economy-in-the-netherlands-by-2050/Circulaire+Economie+EN_v4.pdf

3 See for example Liesbet, H., & Gary, M. (2003). 'Unraveling the central state, but how? Types of multi-level governance'. *American political science review, 97*(02), pp. 233-243.

4 The Finnish initiative 'Design for Government' is an interesting example in this regard, as it is an experimentation agency working from the prime minister's office.

Part Two
Perspectives on Circular Urbanity

Introduction

In Part One, we took a trip through today's circular spiral. First, we learned from an array of pioneering protagonists by collecting basic knowledge about their work, needs and challenges. Next, we framed and contextualized their work by analysing four inspiring approaches at the city and regional level. Finding regulation to be a particularly laborious challenge, and expanding our trip to an even wider perspective, we inspected two national political agendas. In the end, traversing multiple layers of circular city making provided an overview of complex challenges and within-reach opportunities that speak to individuals, communities, civil society, government, industry and everything in between.

In Part Two, we turn to opinions. Experts, professionals, city makers and thinkers present their take on the circular transition. While we are beginning to see circularity being used as marketing, this is only a symptom of our main concern: the process of socio-spatial urban transformation. As it encompasses a number of city-centred challenges from a variety of perspectives, implementing transition schemes requires time and complex organization. In this part, we look into this complex system through the minds of four informed contributors.

Konstantinos Kourkoutas, from the Universitat Autonoma de Barcelona (UAB) looks at Barcelona as an example of a city that makes an effort to metabolize its systems. Federico Savini, from the University of Amsterdam, Department of Geography, Planning and International Development Studies provides an evaluative inspection of Amsterdam's circular approach, looking at how the city is managing a complex socio-economic transition. Michiel Schwarz from Sustainism Lab digs deep into the tricky issues of cultural change, helping us better understand this through a set of more appropriate definitions, formulated to fit a 'sustainist' approach. Last but not least, Joost Beunderman hits on all of the issues above and every matter mentioned in this book, presenting a well-reasoned argument in favour of a more comprehensive, systemic approach to circular city making—including all the not-so-trendy-yet-necessary operations to implement it.

Contemplating the Paradigm Shift Toward a Circular Urban Metabolism Through the Case Study of Ateneus De Fabricación in Barcelona

Konstantinos Kourkoutas
Universitat Autonoma de Barcelona (UAB)

All living systems are capable of metabolizing available energy resources in order to maintain or even increase their levels of organization, which is to say their organized systemic complexity. In the same manner, cities present metabolic and systemic functions similar to natural ecosystems. Notwithstanding the added complexity that the urban context entails, it can be asserted that cities are systems with a proper structure and function, which follow thermodynamic principles and present metabolic functions in the strictest definition of the word; they transform energy.

In this sense, contemporary cities are open systems—not self-contained, and maintained by exchanges of materials, energy and information with areas beyond their region, respectively increasing their internal organization and complexity. In pragmatic terms, no city is sustainable, in the sense of being an autotrophic or even self-supporting ecosystem. Cities will always be heterotrophic systems, since resources and supporting processes must be supplied by ecosystems beyond the formal urban limits. The fact that cities are open, energy-dissipative and heterotrophic systems distinguishes them from natural ecosystems that strive toward energetic auto-sufficiency. Therefore, specifically when referring to cities, the term social ecosystems should be used to make implicit the superposition of cultural infrastructures over the natural ones.

This thermodynamic approach to cities mirrors the essence of urban complexity, which is a consequence of an intermittent interaction between dissipative and homeostatic processes. The repeated cyclical tendency (of social ecosystems) to break the equilibrium (dissipative processes) of the city and to re-establish its initial equilibrium (homeostatic processes) is at the heart of urban transformation as a dynamic process and, as consequence, it constitutes a key aspect of urban metabolism.

Accordingly, cities need to generate and use all available energy and material resources efficiently; mimicking nature´s capabilities of doing so, but also considering their projected impact at larger scales, from regional to global. Urban fabrics should seek to be energy-self-sufficient and close the loops of resource and energy usage, while operating at optimum levels of energy and resource consumption. In this sense, the field of biomimicry offers an inspiration and a basis for the optimal design of urban systems, from buildings to whole city regions. Existing natural ecosystems are examples of self-organized systems with an adaptive capacity developed through evolution, selection, and migration, and therefore provide a substantial and useful database of knowledge for sustainability studies and design at every scale. The need to apply the principle of circular metabolism in urban ecosystems is thus becoming increasingly urgent in order to be able to reduce the urban ecological footprint in an adequate and efficient way, without disrupting key urban functions and components. Applying the principle of circular metabolism on different city scales (region, city, neighbourhood, building) will be key in reducing the ecological footprint at these respective scales in order to achieve a bigger impact. Applying decentralized and low-maintenance solutions that integrate material and energy flows within smaller proximity loops can further increase the complexity of city systems, and thus their overall resilience.

This initial overview of the diverse characteristics and considerations attached to the city concept when rethought as a socio-ecological system was intended to describe the emerging complexity appearing in the contemporary perspective on city processes and dynamics, and also comes to stress the importance of urban metabolism when making reference to circular economy in the urban and territorial context. The case study of the Ateneus de Fabricació network in Barcelona presents an example of a city initiative to tackle this metabolic question on different levels. A network of digital fabrication centres, the initiative is promoted by the administration, but conceived through a bottom-up approach with respect to its development and functioning.

The Ateneus de Fabricació (AdF) network was established in late 2014, initially thought of as an innovative public service where people can collaboratively learn, work, create and turn ideas into realities to help transform the urban environment and contribute to local social development, marking a different trend among all the private and often exclusive fab lab type initiatives. The original aim was to structure and coordinate a strategic project of public participation and empowerment—a 'bottom-up' network based on the precepts of social innovation and collaborative economy, with the goal of tackling a series of societal challenges; first of all, to bring the science and technology of digital manufacturing to all citizens, whether individuals, organizations, businesses, schools or other institutions, while also developing models of participation and networking aimed at promoting social innovation, collaborative economy, new forms of communication, exchange of talent and open learning and sharing, and more importantly, the co-creation of urban environments. The means to achieve this include providing support for local projects, especially ones that have a social return and impact for specific social groups and collectives, within the neighbourhood, city, or whole world, and sharing the knowledge generated collectively in all processes. Nevertheless, the ultimate goal of the AdF network is to enable local residents, people who know the city better than anyone, to propose projects and solutions that improve their immediate urban surroundings. All citizens are invited, regardless of origin, training, gender, profession or age; all are free to form a group and propose a project. It is exactly this diversity and the sum of the different talents that contribute to the collective wealth of the emerging ecosystem around each AdF.

Apart from the initial goal of social innovation, it was soon realized by the administration that the network could achieve a great impact in environmental terms, fostering a new culture of reparation, reutilization, efficient design and environmental sensitivity throughout the urban fabric. The fact that one of the AdFs (Barceloneta) is located within the Fabrica del Sol, a municipal environmental education centre, promoted this idea even further. In early 2016, a participative workshop with municipal technicians, academics and citizens was held in order to co-define the strategic development lines for the AdF network, with respect to the network's functioning. Apart from the challenges mentioned earlier, a series of objectives related to the principles of circular metabolism and economy were introduced that enhanced the initial perspective. The departing point was the need for a paradigm shift in order to be able to change the societal perception of what is now considered, generically speaking, as waste, to what can potentially become a future resource. In this sense, the AdFs set the objective to work with the material waste of their immediate surroundings, while promoting the reparation and reutilization of assets and materials and facilitating the creation of innovative solutions. And in this process of fabrication, introduce principles of eco-design, consider the lifecycle analysis of products and processes, and seek efficiency in terms of material, energy and transport. Of course multiple design questions came into play, but more importantly a critical question was raised—that of creating and fostering a local, productive design culture: a culture that embodies collaborative work, makes efficient use of its local resources and produces artefacts that have a personal and social impact.

For its functioning, the AdF network chose to adopt a collaborative model of economy, which is based more on the concept of use than of property or ownership, considering that sharing itself can be a model for a business, a city, and/or a modus vivendi. The starting point is that the use of the AdFs (spaces, machines and people) is subjected to a system of compensations in terms of knowledge and service trade-offs. The trade-offs are meant to act as a social return to the AdF, the people or the city, by the users who have been given support to develop a project through the AdF network. It is meant to generate additional complexity around the AdF network, creating an emerging ecosystem with exponential growth, multiplying the network's potential resources and adding additional resilience. But it is also meant to work as a catalyst for the emergence of innovative and socially responsible business models and an applied circular economy paradigm as a complementary layer of the circular metabolism scheme.

In parallel, the AdF network has initiated an ample range of educational programmes aimed at promoting social innovation and environmental education of the local citizens, actively reaching out to schools, families and, in general, potential innovators of the city as preferential groups that should be able to enjoy an innovative space to learn, train and develop their talents collaboratively.

In this first period, a considerable amount of work was done, but there are still key issues to be resolved and challenges that need to be tackled in order for the Adf network to achieve an even wider impact. These are challenges related to the sustainability of the network in general and specific terms; economic—ensuring the necessary funding for the long-term sustainability of the project and its future expansion; environmental—reducing the overall environmental footprint of the network and of the citizens; and social—eliminating exclusion of lower social classes from digital fabrication technologies and empowering emerging collectives and professionals. And then there are issues related to functional aspects of the network; such as the centres' material supply from local sources and their functional linkage with local recycling centres, which implies resolving a series of legal frameworks inhibiting this linkage; changing society's mindset and actively instilling principles of collaboration and circular economy into everyday life through education; and the ongoing process of expanding the network to a citywide level, in order to achieve the maximum possible impact while at the same time seeking synergies and complementarities with local dynamics. Because in coordination with similar local initiatives (fab labs, makers, hackers & designers, etc.), AdF is better able to start giving form and structure to a citywide ecosystem that is radically challenging how we make the city, as well as how we relate to it as citizens.

Given the brief period that the network has been in function, it is too early to perform an adequate analysis that can fairly consider all factors in play. But it is important to stress the strategic importance that the municipality has allocated to the AdF network as a societal and environmental catalyst in the ongoing democratization and digital social innovation processes on a citywide level. Combined with the demonstrated potential of its first stage, AdF creates a promising perspective for a real social transformation that we will need to keep our eyes on. As the AdF network continues with the intent of incorporating circularity principles and expanding them on a citywide level, it aspires to provide a demonstrated paradigm shift towards a new era of urban ecology and economy.

All living cities metabolize available energy resources in order to sustain themselves or grow even further. Our built cities are results and products of their social metabolism, manifested in a built physical environment, the management of material and energy resources and a social dynamic that dictates the use of these resources. As cities grow, facilities such as the AdF can help them tackle the aforementioned issues efficiently while increasing their levels of organization, integrating the dissipative traces of social metabolism and creating in parallel new business and economic opportunities. Framed by the adequate legal and policy frameworks, such networks can bring significant and radical transformation to the existing linear metabolic functioning of cities, introducing elements of circularity and additional resilience to the entire urban fabric.

———

References

Acebillo, Josep Antoni. *The New Urban Metabolism: Barcelona.* ACTAR Publishers, 2011.

Ateneus de fabricació. http://ateneusdefabricacio.barcelona.cat. Accessed 17 Jan. 2017.

Childers, Daniel L., et al. "Advancing urban sustainability theory and action: Challenges and opportunities." Landscape and Urban Planning 125 (2014): 320-328.

Fitxes estat XAF, IMI-BCN, Agost, 2016. Internal document.

Odum, Howard T. "Self-Organization, Transformity, and Information." Science 242.4882 (1988): 1132-1139.

Pickett, S. T. A., et al. "Ecological science and transformation to the sustainable city." Cities 32 (2013): S10-S20.

Rueda, Salvador. Barcelona, ciudad mediterránea, compacta y compleja: una visión de futuro más sostenible. Ayuntamiento de Barcelona, 2007.

Tarpuna Coop. Sessions de fabricació sostenible: La Fàbrica del Sol: Gener-Febrer. 2016.

Terradas, Jaume. Ecología urbana. 2001.

Wasted Experiments: A Commentary on Amsterdam Policy for a Circular Society

Federico Savini
University of Amsterdam,
Department of Geography, Planning
and International Development Studies

Over the last ten years, Amsterdam has showed itself to be a city with great energy, an active imagination for a better and more sustainable future, and a very engaged and entrepreneurial civic society that is busy in all kinds of sustainable projects in and for the city. Building on decreasing real estate investments after the bubble burst, many local entrepreneurs, small and medium-sized companies and resourceful citizens have engaged in an urban brainstorm about a possible future made of creative environmental practices, reuse and a growing green economy. As a result, circularity has taken central stage as one of the most evocative and inspiring ideas for this environmental activism. Today, it is really impossible to ignore the fact that circularity, intended as the reuse of all wasted resources of our individual and collective living, is a powerful idea to trace a vision of an urban future that seriously considers long-lasting adaptation to climate without underestimating the need for a healthy economy.

Looking closely, we see a broad set of experimental initiatives inspired by circularity— from reusing discarded clothes to producing biogas from garden waste, and from recycling wasted food into sexy restaurant menus to reintegrating waste-water nutrients into the agri-food production chain. These activities are all praised as 'experiments' in an active, green urban system. Environmental studies look at them as 'niches' for future ecological institutions, or as 'laboratories' for meaningful socio-economic interactions. And they definitely are—these local experiences are in fact fertile ground for a more sustainable urban economy and society. They offer a new understanding of the idea of 'waste' and redefine the idea of 'resource'. Yet, how can these wonderful narratives and concrete spatial experiments radically change our cities?

Amsterdam officials and politicians have rapidly picked up these emerging socio-economic practices to trigger a process of institutional, legal, financial and governmental change. The first step was to include local stakeholders in a process of dialogue in order to better sketch the socio-economic and spatial barriers and opportunities for a circular city. In the policy document *Circular Amsterdam* and in the earlier *Agenda duurzaamheid* ('Sustainability Agenda'), the municipality outlined an action plan to 'govern' this socio-economic transition. The conclusions of this document are quite straightforward and, unfortunately, not very innovative compared to all the policy documents produced over the last ten years (or even since the 1990s). First, it is recognized that there are two main recurrent barriers to the full realization of a circular economy in the city: the non-adaptive legal frameworks and a culture of linear production based on supply-consume-waste models. Existing laws are accused of increasing 'uncertainty' for incoming investors, while the established culture (of the people, administrators and companies) is considered an obstacle for rethinking the way of collecting, transferring, managing and reusing waste. The document proposes two equally simplistic solutions to this problem: first, the establishment of some rule-free zones, considered to provide an incentive to new circular start-ups in the city, and second, more investments in technological innovation, considered to give easier access to information and faster communication, which in turn reduces investment 'risks' in the reuse of waste. In sum, this proposes deregulation and informatization according to the belief that old rules do not work and must be removed, and that old cultures do not work and must be changed through better and more informed communication.

These two approaches to circularity are not innovative and actually insufficient in two ways. First, they exclusively address the need to activate experiments, rather than seriously discuss their institutionalization at broad levels. Transition studies have frequently revealed that the governmental embedding of experiments is a first, important step in enabling transitions, but it is also self-evident that this is not enough to carry out substantial institutional change. Secondly, the two proposed circular solutions tend to exaggerate the capacity of entrepreneurial actors and new companies to change the urban economy. The municipality of Amsterdam basically affirmed the illusion that better communication technologies will institutionalize circularity in the entire city. However, it is also self-evident that more experiments and more communication do not necessary lead to a radical change in the whole urban system of production and consumption.

Consequently, current policy in Amsterdam appears to underestimate the importance of the broad institutional conditions for nurturing and sustaining experiments in circularity. We can distinguish between two specific challenges for governments when tackling the problem of institutionalizing experiments. The first (and the easier to agree with) is the need to provide opportunities for experimentation in the city. Better regulations (not less) and technology are certainly useful for this purpose. The second (and the most difficult to name explicitly) is to start eroding linear economic sectors, which depend on infinitely producing unused waste and exist as the 'main' polluters of our environment. This second point has not yet been found in the policies enacted by the municipality of Amsterdam, which, in my opinion, are not yet mature enough to support a truly circular (r)evolution.

As an example, let us look at how the added economic value of a circular economy is calculated by the City of Amsterdam. Most of the production chains investigated in the *Circular Amsterdam* document are limited to Amsterdam and its metropolitan area. Amsterdam is portrayed as a closed system, where circularity can (easily?) be implemented, and where everybody can gain from it. Yet, there is almost no recognition of the fact that 60% of the 10 million tons of material consumed in the city are fossil fuels coming from outside the city. It is impossible to ignore the fact that Amsterdam's waste is based on an energy and food production chain that goes far beyond the borders of its region. The mass economy of food chain products, packaging and logistic is sustained by a network of companies and interests that have nothing, or almost nothing, to gain from circularity. The same problem applies to the building industry (another pilot case study of Amsterdam's current policy diagnosis); this sector is dominated by international companies and investors that, at the time of booming real estate in the city, are primarily looking for large-scale, rapid supply rather than reusing their waste products.

I believe that a policy for circularity that does not consider the current linear economy's rooted problems and only focuses on experimentation, is not mature. Circularity needs more. And in fact, Amsterdam's entrepreneurial society has demonstrated to be rather well-equipped and motivated to experiment with practices of sharing and reuse. A good system of monetary incentives and physical spaces can already be enough for experiments to proliferate. Instead of more circular experiments, what is needed is a system of disincentives addressing the extensive production of useless waste in the first place, by the players whose economic status depends on wasteful consumption habits. These are large energy corporations, food distributors and packaging producers (and their materials), which in fact base their business model on the very production of waste. These economies of scale are unsuited for the closed-loop systems of circularity, and are actually hindering the innovative potential of experiments.

The City of Amsterdam's current policy ambitions show insufficient awareness of this problem. On the one hand, the municipality is aiming to decrease CO_2 emissions by 45% by 2025; on the other, it intends to do so by promoting energy efficiency in schools, by setting up a fund of 170 million euros, increasing the energy efficiency standard for social housing (which is decreasing in Amsterdam) and increasing electric mobility in the city. Little is said about the need to reuse harbour waste, manage broad growth agendas, increase low pollutant activities instead of fossil-intensive industry (such as harbour aviation). A circular economy needs a policy that deliberately, convincingly and explicitly argues for decentred energy production systems, and for an economy that carefully appreciates the need and social costs of waste.

Circularity is not a creative idea for creative people to freely play with. The way the city is addressing circularity seems to overemphasize the innovative potential of active citizens and their small companies. However, systemically integrating the production chain requires a more consistent and courageous economic, urban and environmental policy. Circularity provides a substantial vision on the political, cultural and economic transition of our society. For this reason, it requires an equally serious vision of structural change. If we do not develop such a vision, we will have a city full of disconnected experiments that will forever remain experiments. And these are wasted experiments.

─────

References

Amsterdam Duurzaam, Agenda voor duurzame energie, schone lucht, een circulaire economie en een klimaatbestendige stad, vastgesteld door de Gemeenteraad van Amsterdam op 11 maart 2015

Bastein, A. G. T. M., et al. "Circular Amsterdam: A vision and action agenda for the city and metropolitan area." TNO, 2016.

From Examples to Exemplars: How Not To Waste the Teachings of Circular City Making in the Sustainist Era

Michiel Schwarz
Sustainism Lab

'Circular city making' is a contested term. Rightly so, because in the current era of 'sustainist' culture we are collectively finding out what circularity could entail, and what we wish it to be. Viewing the interesting display of cases presented in this volume begs the question of how practices can be connected and what their common features are. Before we rush to conclusions about what we can learn from the various cases, it is important to be aware that whatever notion of circularity is adopted, we need to take a stance. Without a perspective on where we are, and where we may be heading, it will be hard to gauge how we can move towards a learning curve on the basis of current practice. We need to take a position as to where we stand vis-à-vis 'circularity', and be analytical. My point of view stems from what I have called 'sustainist culture'. Designating the current era as sustainist (after 20th-century modernist and postmodernist culture), we can observe the emergence of a new ethos and new communities of practice. This cultural shift—of which the idea of placemaking and city making are important signifiers—looks at a future for our living environment and our communities that is more connected, more localized, more collaborative, more human scale, as well as more environmentally sustainable. In this context, the emergent interest in circular city making can be seen as a feature of a shift toward sustainist (design) practice. This sustainist perspective (which I have been developing over the last several years) shifts our focus toward qualities and values for social sustainability and social design, thereby recasting the very meaning of 'sustainability' and 'circularity'.[1] It moves us beyond the technical and the biological, and explicitly incorporates and integrates the social and the human.

The People Dimension in Urban Ecosystems

Creating 'circular cities' involves viewing the urban environment as an integrated system of relationships. Yet, in many of the circular models to date, the technical and the physical have dominated while the social and human dimensions have often been absent in our flow charts and resource loops. From a sustainist perspective, we require a more integrative approach, more encompassing and closer to the original idea of 'ecological'—going back to the Greek word 'oikos', the household—being concerned with interactions between organisms and the environment. After all, we humans—you and me, and all of us—belong as much to our ecologies as do our biological organisms and physical processes. Hence they (we) need to feature much more explicitly on our flow maps, in our circular designs, and in our developing practice of circular city making.

When we re-view circular city making through such a 'sustainist lens', it doesn't take much to distinguish between the cases that are actually incorporating social attributes and human factors in the equation, and those that are limiting the circular system to technical and physical (resource) flows. Looking at some of the cases presented earlier in this volume: realizing a space for borrowing, sharing and learning with your community, as happens, for example, in the London-based 'Library of Things', clearly embodies a very different set of qualities—such as human encounters and dialogue—than those involved in a more technically-driven circular project like a biomeiler system to produce heat from organic waste. Likewise, at the institutional level we can distinguish between the strategies and policy prescriptions that include the civic economy and citizen participation, and those limited to technical, physical and infrastructural solutions.

――――

Collective Learning

What is required, is to develop modes of collective learning that take into account both physical and people flows in a single frame, and to develop circular city making strategies accordingly. This also implies connecting to current urban developments such as the emergence of the so-called 'civic economy' to the idea of circular urbanism.[2] In doing so, we need to enhance our collective learning. How can we begin to draw the lessons from city making experiences in the circular economy? We can continue to collect empirical data, gathering more examples as they emerge almost daily in contemporary urban culture. But sooner rather than later, we will have to move beyond individual case studies and raise a crucial question: 'When do examples become exemplars?'

The difference between an example and an exemplar lies in their scope and share-ability. An example is illustrative of a case, whilst an exemplar is an example that deserves to be reproduced and shared. For a case to be exemplary, it needs to have attributes that are both worthy and adaptable in different contexts. Exemplars provide us with a kind of template, embodying some essential features to be incorporated in future designs elsewhere. Exemplars give us cues as to what is worthwhile to be replicated, both in content and in process. Our collective challenge in the emerging practice of circular city making is to learn and recognize when a case can become exemplary. This is no easy task, but to raise the very question is the first step toward embarking on a learning curve for circular city making. The issue of learning and capacity building is in essence a human challenge, not a technical question. To ask how we can move from examples to exemplars challenges us to develop the skills and tools to gauge how essential features of circular city making can be recreated, propagated and shared.

Building on exemplars is a strategy that is based on building capacity in human terms. In my sustainist view of circular city making, this implies focusing less on being 'smart' by reproducing the technical features of circular systems, and far more on people and communities connecting, learning and sharing. At the heart of the people dimension of circular city making are communities of practice. Learning from exemplars in a way that befits city making in a sustainist mode implies that we place doing before theoretical models. This is exactly what we can see happening in recent trends, where practice is increasingly getting ahead of theory. So rather than putting all our efforts in finding the best theoretical models of circularity, which are subsequently applied in the 'real world' (the old way), it now is emerging praxis in the 'real world' that is giving us the cues for finding appropriate tools and systems for circular city making (the new way). I view this all as part of a sustainist cultural shift, from knowledge to know-how, and from blueprints to shareable experiences.

———

Building on Exemplars: Advancing the Practice of Circular City Making

Learning and sharing are perhaps the key challenges we face in advancing the practice of circular city making. As we begin to develop the ability to identify what deserves to be an exemplar, we need to ask how we can build on these through collective learning and collective innovation.[3] How can we enhance the reach of circular city making? As we address this question, we need to acknowledge that pioneering circular city making cases that have embraced social as well as environmental sustainability, have largely been community-driven, bottom-up and small-scale. So how can we connect the small, often experimental, niche practice of circular city making to the larger systemic level?

Building capacity in circular city making is not a matter of 'upscaling' in the conventional sense. Nor is it an economic issue, but first and foremost a social and cultural one.

Again, it's about learning and sharing, between people and communities. To enhance the body of practice in circular city making requires new approaches. And, I contend, also new terms. The old ways of 'upscaling', by simply growing in volume or multiplying the same identical solutions, is no longer appropriate in the locally embedded practice of city making. More often than not, the civic-driven, neighbourhood-led initiatives depend on a small-scale and nearness for their success, benefiting from what some have called 'dividends of proximity'.[4] These cases frequently depend on local social networks and communities, and such human and social factors are simply not as easily transferable as technical elements.

The key lies not in simple enlargement or duplication. Many civic projects that are working in one area can be shown to also have potential elsewhere. As the in-depth study 'Designed to Scale' by the UK-based Civic Systems Lab concluded about their citizen-led participatory projects in the London borough of Lambeth: "This type of scaling is a proliferation, i.e. the adoption and adaptation of an idea or core model in new contexts, rather than the original project necessarily expanding."[5]

Such a model taps into the networked nature of learning and development. Perhaps the very words 'scaling' and 'upscaling' are misleading. It is the capacity and reach of the whole system, which is made to grow in a networking way. Individual elements in the network are limited in scale, but in their connections, they effectively scale up. This is exactly what is happening in the growth of the civic economy, as witnessed by the growing number of local, citizen-driven initiatives that can be labelled as circular city making. We may call this the micro-infrastructure of sustainist urbanism. A key question is how to connect this to the existing macro-infrastructural projects and policies that now make up the mainstream of designing our cities and neighbourhoods. And, again, I view this first and foremost as a 'people' challenge—social and cultural—not an economic, technological one.

––––––

Circular City Making as Sustainist Design Challenge

Taking a sustainist view has us focus more specifically on a capacity-building approach to circular city making. In doing so, it not only connects with the cultural transition we are experiencing in our cities, but it also recasts circularity as more of a social design challenge. Looking at circular city making through a 'sustainist lens', we see that many of the cases featured in this volume, display the attributes and qualities of what I have termed 'sustainist design'. In our 2013 Sustainist Design Guide, Diana Krabbendam and I have begun to identify a number of sustainist qualities that we argue need to be addressed in our future design briefs: connectedness, sharing, localism and proportionality.[6] Such qualities can be taken as signifiers of circularity, whereby social values are integrated with environmental sustainability concerns. They make us aware that value concerns need explicit attention in the further development of circular design. They may not provide us with an exhaustive set of attributes, but they do refocus our view of what a more community-driven, sustainist mode of circular city making could entail.

––––

Circular Urbanism: Reweaving the Urban Fabric

What all this suggests is that to create transitions towards circular city making on a larger scale requires strategies whereby people and communities can connect, collaborate and share. It also emphasizes that the nexus between local 'niche' and top-down 'mainstream' approaches should be designed and scaled from the local practice upward, and not the other way around. Looking ahead, I contend that the most successful exemplars of circular city making will not be those that treat the local as a smaller version of larger citywide solutions, but rather those that embrace the locally derived, people-centred solutions as root forms that can be multiplied, shared and networked with other (local) communities across the city. Here, 'the city' is recast as a collection of interconnected neighbourhoods and communities.

My sustainist take on circular city making also raises the question of how we can take 'neighbourhood ecology' as our starting point for charting and designing what a circular city making approach could yield, rather than adopting macro level models of the circular city.[7] It also reminds us that new forms of engagement with citizens, communities, and inhabitants are essential. This calls for putting efforts into stimulating a 'participatory ecology'[8], especially at the local scale, to make the circular city in and with local communities.

More broadly, what this implies is that we need to fundamentally re-think how circular city making connects to social change, the civic economy, community collaboration, the local and the small-scale. This poses a deeply social and cultural challenge, whereby a 'sustainist perspective' can give us some pointers and lines of sight. It amounts to no less than a redesign of the 'urban fabric'. In other words, employing the urban fabric metaphor here, we need to develop and connect new and old threads and strands, creating knotted tapestries and diverse weaves rather than uniform cloth, as we re-weave the patterns of urban life. There are no quick production tools at hand to realize this. Today, we are just beginning to recast our models and to redesign our 'looms'—as we aim to create circular places and communities in our cities and our neighbourhoods.

References

Ahrensbach, T., et al. "Compendium for the civic economy: What the big society should learn from 25 trailblazers." *London: 00:/in association with NESTA & Design Council CABE* (2011).

Civic Systems Lab. "Designed to scale: Mass participation to build resilient neighbourhoods." The Open Works/Civic Systems Lab/ Participatory City, 2015, http://www.participatorycity.org/report-the-research. Accessed 17 Jan. 2017.

Leadbeater, Charles. *We-think*. Profile books, 2009.

Montgomery, Charles. *Happy city: transforming our lives through urban design*. Macmillan, 2013.

Schwarz, Michiel. *A Sustainist Lexicon: Seven entries to recast the future — Rethinking design and heritage*. 2016.

Schwarz, Michiel, and Diana Krabbendam. *Sustainist Design Guide*. 2013.

Schwarz, Michiel, and Joost Elffers. *Sustainism is the New Modernism: A Cultural Manifesto for the Sustainist Era*. DAP, 2010.

Wijkecologie Wildeman: Onderzoek naar ontwerpen voor delen als sleutel in de circulaire stad. www.nieuwwestexpress.nl/nl/page/9693/ wijkecologie-wildeman. Accessed 17 Jan. 2017.

———

Notes

1 Following the publication of my 2010 'Sustainism manifesto' with Joost Elffers, coining the word, the sustainist perspective has been developed further in different contexts, involving collaborations with Diana Krabbendam, Jogi Panghaal, Riemer Knoop and others. Michiel Schwarz, Joost Elffers. *Sustainism Is the New Modernism: A Cultural Manifesto for the Sustainist Era* (New York: D.A.P. Distributed Art Publishers, 2010). Michiel Schwarz & Diana Krabbendam, with The Beach network S*ustainist Design Guide: How sharing, localism, connectedness and proportionality are creating a new agenda for social design* (Amsterdam:. BIS Publishers, 2013). Michiel Schwarz, *A Sustainist* Lexicon*: Seven entries to recast the future — Rethinking design and heritage.* With field notes by Riemer Knoop and sustainist symbols by Joost Elffers (Amsterdam: Architectura & Natura Press, 2016).

2 See for example 00:/, *Compendium for the Civic Economy: What our cities, towns and neighbourhoods can learn from 25 trailblazers* (Haarlem, Netherlands: Valiz/Trancity, 2012).

3 Leadbeater's notions of 'we-think' and 'mass participation' are relevant here. Charles Leadbeater, We-Think: Mass innovation, not mass production (London: Profile Books, 2009).

4 Charles Montgomery, *Happy City: Transforming our lives through urban design* (London: Penguin Random House, 2013).

5 Civic Systems Lab, *Designed to Scale*. Mass participation to build resilient neighbourhoods (London: The Open Works/Civic Systems Lab/Participatory City, 2015), http://www.participatorycity.org/report-the-research/

6 Michiel Schwarz & Diana Krabbendam, with The Beach network *Sustainist Design Guide: How sharing, localism, connectedness and proportionality are creating a new agenda for social design* (Amsterdam: BIS Publishers, 2013).

7 This idea is at the core of the 'Wijkecologie' (Neighbourhood Ecology) project in the Wildeman area in Amsterdam Nieuw-West, conducted by The Beach, Ponec de Winter architects, Amsterdam Smart City and Michiel Schwarz/Sustainism Lab. 'Wijkecologie Wildeman: Onderzoek naar ontwerpen voor delen als sleutel in de circulaire stad. https://www.nieuwwestexpress.nl/nl/page/9693/wijkecologie-wildeman.

8 This term is taken from the above-mentioned study Designed to Scale (2015)

The Circular City:
A Systems Challenge,
not a Start-up Story

Joost Beunderman
Architecture00

The great examples in this book are testament to the phenomenal creativity, energy and drive that entrepreneurial people bring to bear on the extraordinary and interrelated challenges our cities face. But they also show how vulnerable many of these initiatives are, operating in what often seems a hostile context where the value that they create (or the future costs they avoid) is not always understood, acknowledged or accounted for, let alone adequately monetized. It's a truism that start-ups struggle with resources, but the nascent circular city, in particular, frequently seems stuck in a scarcity trap.

Beyond the individual case studies and their development pathways, this points to a key issue that is too often misunderstood or downplayed: deep urban transformation is not about a series of great stories on passionate and inventive start-ups, but about systems change. This may be an obvious point, but we live in a world where we hear endless stories about how disruptive start-ups are changing the world. So it's easy to forget that start-ups, while they undeniably have transformational impact, are just one part of a complex picture. To thrive, all such initiatives require an institutional infrastructure fit for the 21st century—where the direct and indirect impact of new economic activities can be made more widely intelligible and valued, made accountable and embedded in contracts. Equally, our collective understanding of resource and material flows and of how our choices impact on them is still rudimentary—and the adjective 'collective' is key here, in order to overcome the niche element of emergent practice, and instead turn this into the new normal. The initiatives chronicled in this book need this to happen to succeed, and therefore they need to take an active part in shifting and shaping this new institutional context.

This needs to be rooted in the fundamental realization that meaningful progress on intractable and wicked social issues in the 21st century can no longer be talked about as the responsibility or capability of a single actor, organization, institution, domain or start-up. Again this seems self-evident, yet the human brain seems hardwired to prefer the simplicity of clear cause-effect stories and silver bullets over complexity, and we see this in the dominant discourses on urban transformation. While the 20th century was dominated by the unhelpful state-market dichotomy, right now the collective imagination seems to be hung up on the Ubers, Teslas and their civic equivalents—be they FabLabs, Incredible Edibles or energy coops. The age of the large state, the heroic business leader or charismatic start-up founder has led to a convenient set of truths about development, investment, accountability and governance. But acting effectively in a 21st-century context requires multi-actor coalitions, whether at the scale of neighbourhoods, city regions or beyond. So what we really need is a more sophisticated collective understanding of how change can happen, not through a series of singular ventures that compete for resources and attention, but through fostering broad coalitions of start-ups, self-producing citizen collectives, government, innovative city mayors, corporates, community organizations, NGOs and financiers working together. As the economist and chronicler of the commons Elinor Ostrom put it in her 2009 Nobel Prize lecture: "We need to ask how diverse polycentric institutions help or hinder the innovativeness, learning, adapting, trustworthiness, levels of cooperation of participants, and the achievement of more effective, equitable, and sustainable outcomes at multiple scales."

Consider an example from beyond the world of the circular production: the case of Ashoka fellow Piyush Tewari, whose crusade against road deaths in India saw him first campaigning for regulatory change (and obtaining a ruling from the courts), and then establishing a programme for organizational culture change within the police to make them more effective actors to deal with people wounded in road accidents. Finally, he co-developed a legislative proposal forcing toll roads to obtain insurance for accidents, and ultimately, worked with a tech company to develop a mobile phone app that reports incidents. Crucially, the app came last, not first—as the issue is systemic and—as much as start-up land tempts us to think that 'whatever the problem, the answer's an app'—reducing road accident deaths cannot be solved by shooting a single arrow.

In his TEDx talk 'Don't be an entrepreneur, build systems', Oxford academic Marc Ventresca pointed out that the language and imagery of entrepreneurship doesn't always help—because creating new value is fundamentally about assembling a series of heterogeneous elements to make sure they align, rather than doggedly pursuing a singular business idea. For example, he shows how the electrification of the western world from the mid-1880s onward wasn't really about exceptionally heroic entrepreneurs building muscular businesses. It was their capacity to be system builders that made their work last—they created coalitions of established and new stakeholders, turned the regulatory system upside down, created new multi-actor protocols and entirely new finance products to enable this world to be created, while at the same time actively, albeit gradually, dismantling the 'legacy system' of gaslight and steam engines. The tragedy now is that we seem to want to engage 21st-century challenges with an industrial-age institutional mindset and narrative of change.

Practically, this means that the perspective of the circular city requires us to work on many levels. Just to name a few, we have to:

———

Work towards greater supply chain transparency, not just through abstract data but also as compelling stories to show the interdependencies between the stuff we buy and the global effects of sourcing them, in the way that Fairphone has helped us understand how obscure metals such as tungsten can be sourced either responsibly or irresponsibly in the Great Lakes region of Africa.

Communicate the circular city as an attractive vision beyond the already-converted crowd. Recently, I heard once again the tiresome story of how a social enterprise collecting and reselling white goods such as refrigerators, in this case in Glasgow, finds it near-impossible to sell them to relatively deprived households who could benefit from the excellent prices they offer—merely because of a negative association with 'charity', whereas environmentally-focused, high-earning households snap them up.

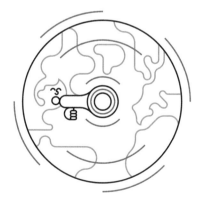

Reimagine our tax system to rebalance the consumption of new goods versus reuse, like the Swedish government has recently announced in an effort to promote the repair economy, sharing economy and (re)making movement, aiming to create lots of low- and medium-skilled jobs in the process.

Imagine and build new ways to invest in systems change rather than just in individual start-ups— based on the social and environmental costs we could avoid through the circular city, rather than being solely focused on the revenue streams from clearly defined individual products and services. The growing FabCity network, initiated by the Institute for Advanced Architecture of Catalonia, the MIT's Center for Bits and Atoms (which incubated the first FabLab) and the Fab Foundation (the global network of FabLabs) may be a vehicle for such a systems-wide view. This network is still young, but it could become an effective platform to bring coalitions together, building a global infrastructure and knowledge source for the radical transformation of how we work, live and play in cities. Interestingly, in signing up cities and regions worldwide, it explicitly invites them to see this as a 40-year transformational journey...

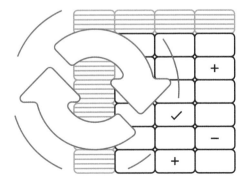

Create new quality assurance, insurance and contract types enabling the en-masse trading of recycled, upcycled or remade products, just like the metals and plastic recycling industries already have intricate coding systems for scrap of various kinds, equally understood in US scrapyards or in Chinese ports, and in family-run or industrial processing plants.

This stuff is the 'dark matter' of systems change—not as eye-catching as individual start-up stories, but necessary if cities are to have dense networks of new ventures, overlapping people and knowledge networks behind these initiatives, funders that 'get it' at a deep and long-term level, and an evolving role of the public sector to support and collaboratively regulate all this. We need both the hyper-local, people-focused, real-world engagements such as WASTED, the Library of Things and the Brighton Waste House, and their invisible, geeky translations to the system world of legislation and finance. It is in the interplay between transparency expectations, tax systems, cultural norms, contract types and investment products that collective expectations start to shift, the threshold to new venturing and investment begins to lower, and new ideas of defining success are developed. In some sense, that age-old icon of Silicon Valley did precisely this—following a series of boom-and-bust rounds, it now dominates the current economic cycle as it defined a discourse and created a new normal, for better or worse. In contrast, the circular city seems a ways away from being the new normal—but we can't afford to see it as a fringe movement.

[This article builds on a body of thought developed together with my colleagues of Dark Matter Laboratories, a 00 studio focused on exploring institutional infrastructures fit for the 21st century.]

References

Dark Matter Labs. http://darkmatterlabs.org. Accessed 17 Jan. 2017.

Ostrom, Elinor. "Nobel prize lecture: Beyond Markets and States: Polycentric Governance of Complex Economic Systems." Nobel Media AB, 08 Dec. 2009, www.nobelprize.org/nobel_prizes/economic-sciences/laureates/2009/ostrom-lecture.html. Accessed 17 Jan. 2017.

Ventresca, Marc. "Don't Be an Entrepreneur, Build Systems." *YouTube*, uploaded by TEDx Talks, 10 July 2011, https://www.youtube.com/watch?v=I9T3diyqRPg. Accessed 17 Jan. 2017.

Conclusion
Circularity as the Undeniable Common Denominator

Francesca Miazzo
and Mehdi Comeau

CITIES Foundation

The time has come to reflect, opening up to criticism, debate and discussion at the end of our journey.

———

In *An Array of Circular Endeavours*, we learned from today's practitioners and protagonists of circular city making. What did we find? New sharing infrastructures affect life at street level, increasing both human interaction and complexity. To generate wider local involvement, new social contracts are established between different urban communities, arranged according to local circumstances with the goal of creating never-explored ownership arrangements. These approaches affect varied segments of urban life. For example, we have seen them in the energy provision sector and the housing market. New forms of ownership are being implemented for resource management in a number of areas, all following a path created by the 'commons' ideal. In *A Selection of Policy Approaches*, we found that opening up to circularity is not an easy experiment at the city level. Issues such as citizen empowerment are very sensitive to local culture. In areas where policy allows citizens to do so, they are fast-generating a scattered landscape of circular, niche urban pockets. This on-the-ground action is supporting a second stage of the process, where a change in daily routines is further spreading new ideas and propositions. In general, we observed inequality: certain types of citizens have more access to circularity than others. Developing national campaigns targeting the final users—who are engaged as co-creators, co-owners and co-change makers—can support in reaching a wider population to create a more inclusive circular future. A different perspective shares a broad agreement that resource optimization is the circular city's most important and necessary focus. However, it seems that no matter when, how or where—people are the cornerstone of circularity. Without the complexity and nuance of people and human interaction, the circular city would be limited to a beautiful technological exercise that only the few can afford. But citizens are not the only focus. The system has to change. This book is based on this presumption—and throughout it, again and again we find that this change requires an intricate evolution of new practices, beliefs, expectations and standards that penetrate deeply across many levels. Yet such a shared, accepted universal approach does not yet exist. Approaching the circular city is a process that, like many others, will require new regulation, empowerment and education that are tuned to local context.

For the system to change, old systems need to become vulnerable and new systems more open to wider portions of society. And to be realistic, this is going to take a long time. As Federico Savini points out in Part Two, urban circularity remains in its infancy. The concept is young, and such complex, systemic change takes time to evolve, adapt and take irrepressible hold. Given the example of Amsterdam, it becomes clear that even for a city so progressive and so robust with innovative thought and action, the Wasted City's rooted resistance to circular change still dominates. In its youth, circularity has not yet 'come of age', reaching the maturity needed to overcome the 'old' (and not so wise) major systems in place. This is understandable. And it makes sense that Amsterdam and other cities kick-start the transition to circularity by promoting and fostering a very agile, adaptive and innovative approach that empowers any interested citizens, businesses and organizations to experiment. Not to mention the cultural, societal vibrations this type of action produces, which continually shake the outdated pillars holding up the very systems it seeks to topple. This seems far from futile. Yet in the end, more forceful initiative from higher-level actors may be necessary to make those pillars fall. And when they do come down, we'll need a new support system ready to uphold a circular mode of operating and living. In this picture, the more experimentation, the better—as long as it coincides with and precipitates the implementation of bigger, stronger, more systemic initiatives. It did take some 60 years for previous generations to develop today's globally embedded linear system... With this book as the starting point, we begin counting the time until circular city making approaches become the true foundation of new urban systems—even if the transformation takes longer than a lifetime.

In conclusion, this book is not meant to provide circular city making approaches, per se, but rather to facilitate dialogue and action that advance circularity as systemic modus operandi. Accordingly, this book can be used as a tool to inform, advance, integrate and establish support for circular approaches. We envision organizing moments of sharing, where the book's contents are presented and its opinions disputed in order to provide a more contextualized narrative of our findings. In these moments, additional narratives will be created. The statements below are a series of postulations derived from this book, which we hope will be used by present and future generations to ignite and instil yet-to-be-familiar urban operations—where circularity is the undeniable common denominator.

> Ownership is dead, shared infrastructures are the cradle of a new urbanity.

> People are the cornerstone of urban circularity, and you'll never walk alone.

> Regulation must not lag behind the niche. Without new rules, the process is too slow.

> Urban metabolism is screaming for commodity brokers.

> Circular education is paramount for the wider population.

> Circularity is not the sole goal; it is a means for systemic change.

Contributors

CITIES Foundation

—

Francesca Miazzo is CITIES Foundation's managing director and co-founder. Italian, she is based in Amsterdam, where she graduated from the University of Amsterdam's Research Master's Urban Studies. Francesca manages and coordinates CITIES' initiatives, events, studies and projects, including the community-driven, local plastic waste recycling scheme WASTED. Francesca is lead editor, curator, and author of this book's introduction and conclusion.

—

Mehdi Comeau is the director of his writing and communications company, urban ENSŌ, and was CITIES' communication coordinator for over three years. American/French, Mehdi is based in Amsterdam. He graduated *cum laude* from the University of Amsterdam's Urban Sociology MSc, and today works with innovative clients in urbanism, culture and technology. Mehdi copy-edited this book, and co-authored the introduction and conclusion.

—

Alex Thibadoux is a designer and researcher from Tennessee, USA, currently based in Amsterdam as a freelancer. With a background in landscape architecture and urban design, he has a keen interest in how the cityscape influences human behaviour and how cities may evolve in the future. Based on the interviews he conducted, Alex profiles 16 circular initiatives in this book's first section.

Contributors

Marijana Novak is a Master of Sustainable Finance, operating as an independent consultant in the Netherlands. Her work involves the application of risk modelling, quantitative finance and strategic analytics to the creation of a sustainably built environment and transition to the circular economy. In this book, Marijana explores the divergent circular approaches of four different cities.

Anna Hult is an academic and urbanist, completing her PhD in Urban and Regional Studies at the KTH Royal Institute of Technology in Stockholm, with the thesis *Unpacking Swedish Sustainability: the promotion and circulation of sustainable urbanism*. She is also one of CITIES two co-founders. In this book, Anna considers the national approach to circular policy.

Barbara Koole is WASTED's co-initiator and former project manager. As such, she has given numerous presentations and collaborated with academics and professionals nationally and internationally. She has a background in political science and urban policy. In this book, Barbara investigates the role of national governments in establishing a circular city.

Joost Beunderman is a director of Architecture 00, the London-based strategy and design practice. He leads on a wide range of urban strategy, regeneration and research projects. He was the main author of the *Compendium of the Civic Economy*, published in 2011 as an overview of people-powered practice in revitalizing places. Joost is also the Director of Impact Hub Islington and Impact Hub Brixton, two co-working spaces for impact-driven ventures that are part of a global network. He is currently working with 00's Dark Matter Laboratories studio on a range of institutional design projects.

Maarten Hajer is a distinguished professor of Urban Futures at Utrecht University. Before, he was a professor of Public Policy at the University of Amsterdam (1998–2015), Director of the Netherlands Environmental Assessment Agency (PBL—Planbureau voor de Leefomgeving, 2008–2015), and Chief Curator of the 2016 International Architecture Biennale Rotterdam.

Konstantinos Kourkoutas is a PhD recipient at the Urbanism Department of the Universitat Politecnica de Catalunya (UPC) in Barcelona, where he also completed his Master in Architecture. He participated in different national and European research programmes on urban and territorial development while assisting with teaching duties in various urban design courses. Since 2015, he has worked as the coordinator of a multidisciplinary research cluster on Smart and Sustainable Cities, as coordinator of over 35 research groups in the Universitat Autonoma de Barcelona (UAB), and he assists with the strategic development of the university's research areas related to open innovation, living labs and territorial transfer knowledge.

Federico Savini is Assistant Professor in Urban and Regional Planning at the University of Amsterdam. He studies urban development from a political and sociological perspective, focusing on the urban politics of sustainability and the financial-legal challenges of land development.

Michiel Schwarz (Sustainism Lab) is an independent cultural thinker, researcher of the future and consultant. He is the co-creator of the 2010 manifesto *Sustainism Is the New Modernism* (with Joost Elffers; New York) coining the word 'sustainism' for the next cultural paradigm. His most recent publications are *Sustainist Design Guide* (with Diana Krabbendam, 2013) and *A Sustainist Lexicon* (2016). Under the banner of his Sustainism Lab, he is currently developing projects on sustainist culture, including a research collaboration with Reinwardt Academy's Heritage Lab (Amsterdam University of the Arts), and with The Beach social design hub, Amsterdam.

Credits

Circular Endeavour Case Studies

Essays on Policy Approaches

—— 　　　　　　　　　　　——

Colophon

Production

This publication was made possible through the generous support of the Creative Industries Fund NL.

creative industries fund NL

The Wasted City - Approaches to Circular City Making was produced by:

Chief editor
Francesca Miazzo,
CITIES Foundation

Content editor
Mehdi Comeau

Contributors
Francesca Miazzo,
Mehdi Comeau, Alex Thibadoux,
Marijana Novak, Anna Hult,
Barbara Koole, Joost Beunderman,
Konstantinos Kourkoutas,
Federico Savini, Michiel Schwarz

Preface
Maarten Hajer, Distinguished
Professor Urban Futures,
Department of Geo Sciences,
Utrecht University

Book design
Chris Knox (CITIES)

Illustrations
Calvin Sprague, Pavlov Visuals

Proof editing
Leo Reijnen

Prepress
Colorset, Amsterdam

Printing
Wilco, Amersfoort

Contact information

Contact for bookings,
lectures and debates
on circular city making
and systemic urban change:
Ieva Punyte:
ieva@citiesfoundation.org

Publishers
Simon Franke – Trancity,
info@trancity.nl,
www.trancity.nl

Pia Pol,
Astrid Vorstermans – Valiz,
info@valiz.nl,
www.valiz.nl

trancity*valiz is a collaboration
between two independent
publishers that share a common
understanding regarding the
function of publications. Their
books provide critical reflection
and interdisciplinary inspiration,
and establish a connection
between cultural disciplines and
socio-economic issues.

Publications on the city, urban
change and the public domain are
at the core of the collaboration
between Trancity and Valiz.

ISBN 978-94-92095-31-2

© trancity*valiz

Distribution

BE/NL/LU
Coen Sligting
www.coensligtingbookimport.nl

Centraal Boekhuis
www.centraal.boekhuis.nl

GB/IE
Anagram
www.anagrambooks.com

Europe/Asia
Idea Books
www.ideabooks.nl

Australia
Perimeter Books
www.perimeterbooks.com

USA
D.A.P
www.artbook.com

Individual orders
www.trancity.nl
www.valiz.nl